CW01086025

War

Mindset

Affirmations

Powerful Challenges for Men to
Awaken the Inner Badass and
Boost Self-Love

by

Greg Butcher

Relaxed Guru Books

Table of Contents

Introduction

Awaken the Warrior

In this book you will learn how to become your own badass superhero, the warrior you were born to be. You will discover how to tap into an endless source of strength and power that lies within you.

First and foremost, the Warrior Mindset is not about combat or competition; rather it's about taking control of our thoughts, words and actions in order to promote personal growth and development. Inside this book you will learn how to build self-esteem, love yourself and embrace your masculinity. The Warrior Mindset will also help you to erase the limitations that were put on you by other people.

It is much easier to complain about what is wrong with our lives or the world around us, but that's merely an exercise in futility. Instead, you have to look for things in your life that you can be thankful for and try to change what you don't like. That will help you learn how to love yourself and be happy, you will even want to help others that are in need.

You have to understand, that self-love is not selfish, it's about taking care of ourselves so that we can be the best for those around us, especially our loved ones. No matter what challenges you are facing in life, you will be able to conquer them.

Each lesson in this book starts with a challenge that will expand the limits that you inflicted on yourself and help you develop powerful positive mindset. This will ultimately help you to become the best version of yourself.

Repeat the affirmations in this book to help you get motivated and achieve your objectives. These are designed to make you think about what path do you want take, who do you want to be and where your limit really is. They will get longer and more intense as the book progresses. That kind of positive reinforcement will help you to stay focused and not give up at the first hurdle.

I wrote this book for you so you can take control of your fate and live a fulfilling life, eventually becoming the best possible version of yourself. It's about understanding that we all have a choice how we deal with everything in our lives, including ourselves. So do not wait and start right now, choose to take action and empower yourself. Nothing can stop you from achieving what you are truly capable of.

If you believe this book will be helpful to someone you care about, please share it with them!

Lesson I. Purpose

The warrior in you believes in himself - because the only one who can change your life is YOU. He believes that nothing is impossible to those who do not fear failure.

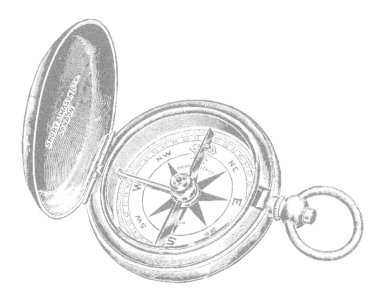

Challenge: Set goals and achieve them

Focus on what you want in life rather than what you are expected to. Create a vision board that displays your goals and dreams and reflects how you hope to change in the future.

To start, take a look at your life and decide what you want to accomplish. Write down your dreams, hopes, and desires on an index card or piece of paper. Your goals may include pushing yourself to work out more often than before or finally asking that girl out on a date. It doesn't matter if it's big or small. What matters is what you want to accomplish in your life. Then, decide on at least three goals that you want to achieve right now.

Once you have them, write the following phrase next to them:

I will set my mind to _____ and follow through with it no matter what.

Follow this phrase up by a plan. For example, "I will work out more often" becomes "I will set my mind to work out three times a week and follow through with it no matter what."

Once you've written these goals down, it's time to set your mind to achieving them. Every morning after getting up, take a look at these phrases and your goals. Remind yourself of the power within you and what you hope to accomplish in life.

Affirmations 1-100

1) I am loved.

2) I am worthy.

3) Life is good.

4) I am a winner.

5) I am handsome.

6) Life loves me.

7) I am attractive.

8) My mind is free.

9) Women admire me.

10) I am a strong man.

11) It's all up to me.

12) Life is wonderful.

13) I am a capable man.

14) I deserve the best.

15) I will win at life.

16) I am a man of valor.

17) I am a money magnet.

18) I celebrate success.

19) I deserve happiness.

20) Life is truly great.

21) The world adores me.

22) I accept success now.

23) I act on my thoughts.

24) I am a confident man.

25) I am a man among men.

26) I am a man of action.

27) I am a success story.

28) I feel healthy today.

29) I see only solutions.

30) My mind can be still.

31) Today is a great day.

32) I am a capable person.

33) I am a high value man.

34) I am a leader at work.

35) I am a man of my word.

36) I value my time alone.

37) The universe loves me.

38) I am a disciplined man.

39) I am a positive person.

40) I am dreaming big today.

41) I command myself to win.

42) I make positive changes.

43) My actions are powerful.

44) People enjoy my company.

45) The future begins today.

46) The future looks bright.

47) What I sow, I will reap.

48) Failure is not an option.

49) I am completely fearless.

50) I am free from all anger.

51) I am now living my dream.

52) My success is inevitable.

53) Success is my birthright.

54) Today is a new beginning.

55) I am a pillar of strength.

56) I am masculine and strong.

57) I am wise beyond my years.

58) I have a lot going for me.

59) I see myself as a success.

60) My abundance is limitless.

61) My mind is clear and calm.

62) My potential is limitless.

63) Success is my only option.

64) Today, I invest in myself.

65) I am the leader of my life.

66) Discipline creates freedom.

67) I am confident and capable.

68) I am free from all anxiety.

69) I am successful in my life.

70) I am the best man I can be.

71) I am the master of my life.

72) I am the sexiest man alive.

73) I deserve the best in life.

74) I deserve to be successful.

75) I have limitless potential.

76) I love to learn new things.

77) Life has never been better.

78) My family supports me 100%.

79) My mind is sharp as a tack.

80) People are happy to see me.

81) Today I am a better person.

82) Today I choose to be happy.

83) Discipline is my superpower.

84) I am a disciplined achiever.

85) I am always making progress.

86) I am happy with what I have.

87) I am in control of my moods.

88) I am masculine and powerful.

89) I am strong and independent.

90) I find happiness in my work.

91) If I say something, I do it.

92) My life is one of abundance.

93) Success is on my path today.

94) I always have plenty of time.

95) I am a kind and powerful man.

96) I am a man and I am powerful.

97) I am charming and attractive.

98) I am everything I want to be.

99) I am open to new experiences.

100) I attract women effortlessly.

02

Lesson II. Serenity

The warrior in you knows where to draw the line - he's smart enough not to fight with an idiot. He doesn't take stupid risks and hates senseless violence. But, when someone comes at him trying to hurt him or his family, he'll never back down from getting his point across.

Challenge: Cultivate a sense of peace and calm

Practice to increase your inner peace and sense of self-worth. Take up a mind-body practice such as mindfulness meditation, yoga, or qi gong to tap into your higher self's tremendous energy and unlock the power within. Learn to quiet your mind and become mindful by practicing being present in the moment or spending time in nature every day.

To start, take a look at your schedule and find just 15 minutes of free time. This could be during the day before work, on your lunch break or after dinner. It doesn't matter where you do it as long as it's somewhere quiet.

Once you have this time set aside, turn off any distractions such as cell phones and sit with your eyes closed. Breathe in and out slowly, noticing each breath as it goes in through your nose and out of your mouth. If thoughts come into your mind about what you have to do later or something stressful that happened earlier, let them pass by without judgment or attachment. It's just part of the meditation process.

Set a daily reminder to take time for yourself to meditate or be mindful of your surroundings. You'll be amazed at how much it helps to cultivate a sense of peace within you.

You can apply mindfulness anytime. Focus on the beauty in every moment. Breathe in a sense of stillness and allow yourself to feel grounded and centered. As you focus your "mind's eye" on what is before you take note of one thing about it that makes it unique from anything else you've ever seen.

Affirmations 101-200

101) I have a right to be wealthy.

102) My creativity is unstoppable.

103) My life is a dream come true.

104) My mind is clear and focused.

105) People are harmless to me.

106) People love me, just as I am.

107) The world supports me now.

108) I am in charge of my own life.

109) I am a genius whenever I work.

110) I am a man who does not judge.

111) I am extremely physically fit.

112) I am good with who I am today.

113) I am safe wherever I go today.

114) I am unique and one of a kind.

115) I choose success over failure.

116) I choose the thoughts, I think.

117) I let myself go and feel free.

118) I take action and get results.

119) Life is so much fun right now.

120) Life supports me at all times.

121) My body is strong and healthy.

122) My thoughts create my reality.

123) My voice is sexy and alluring.

124) Only goodness comes to me now.

125) All around me, success abounds.

126) I am a man of high self-esteem.

127) I am a man of wisdom and power.

128) I am a man that loves his work.

129) I am taking control of my life.

130) I am the master of my thoughts.

131) I choose to be calm and serene.

132) I give 100% to everything I do.

133) I have great people in my life.

134) I have the patience of a saint.

135) I make my thoughts work for me.

136) I radiate peace, love, and joy.

137) If I can dream it, I can do it.

138) Men were created for greatness.

139) My confidence is growing daily.

140) My voice is deep and masculine.

141) The best is yet to come for me.

142) The future looks bright for me.

143) Today is my day; no one else's.

144) Today, all is well in my world.

145) I am a strong and confident man.

146) All of my thoughts are positive.

147) Every day of my life is amazing.

148) I always make the right choices.

149) I am a confident, masculine man.

150) I am a strong, confident person.

151) I am physically fit and healthy.

152) I am tightly coiled male energy.

153) I choose to be happy, right now.

154) I live with purpose and meaning.

155) I love the person I am becoming.

156) Life is good today and every day.

157) Money flows easily into my life.

158) My body is strong and masculine.

159) My income increases every week.

160) My mind is focused on solutions.

161) My work ethic is above reproach.

162) The best in life is yet to come.

163) Time is my friend, not my enemy.

164) Today I can accomplish anything.

165) What I don't know won't hurt me.

166) I speak with purpose and clarity.

167) All negativity is leaving me now.

168) All of my dreams are coming true.

169) As I breathe, so shall I prosper.

170) Everything I touch turns to gold.

171) I am a genius and I am brilliant.

172) I am a man of strength and honor.

173) I am deeply interested in myself.

174) I am filled with self-confidence.

175) I am now grateful for everything.

176) I am proud of my accomplishments.

177) I am successful in all that I do.

178) I deserve to be rich and wealthy.

179) I don't have time for negativity.

180) I have a strong and healthy body.

181) I use my strength to help others.

182) If others are doing it, so can I.

183) If you want something, go get it.

184) Life is exciting and adventurous.

185) My ability to focus is unlimited.

186) My muscles get bigger by the day.

187) My past does not equal my future.

188) My success in life is inevitable.

189) The only thing I fear is failure.

190) The world is mine for the taking.

191) Today is going to be a great day.

192) Today, all goes well in my world.

193) Today, I am overflowing with joy.

194) What's in my mind is in my power.

195) All of my problems have solutions.

196) Every day is better than the last.

197) Fear can never hold me back again.

198) I am a man of clear understanding.

199) I am a man of unsurpassed courage.

200) I am a man who refuses to give up.

03

Lesson III. Obstacles

The warrior in you will never give up - not on any obstacle that stands between him and his dreams (a better life, more money, a healthy family, an enviable lifestyle). He has the courage to take risks and the tenacity to see things through.

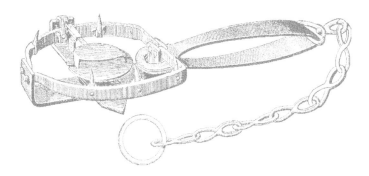

Challenge: Focus on your goals

Stay focused on your goals and what you want to achieve in life. Do not lose sight of your goals and the steps to achieve them. It is very easy for life's distractions and demands to take center stage, but you must stay focused on all that you want to achieve in life.

To start, look at your written goals from challenge one. How are you doing on your goals? Are you keeping up with them daily? Or have they already become just another to-do list that has fallen to the bottom of the pile?

Now, write down what is getting in the way of you accomplishing your goals. Is it an addiction like smoking, eating out too much or watching too much TV? Is it laziness, lack of motivation or low self-esteem?

Once you have identified the obstacles, write down how many times a day they are getting in your way. Then, write down your solution to bust through them so that your goals become achievable again. Write it down in the following format:

I will achieve my goal to _____ by doing _____.

For example, "I will achieve my goal to start eating healthier by eating one fruit and one vegetable at every meal."

Take action today to achieve your goals. As you start transitioning into a new way of life, these obstacles will begin to dissipate as you become more conscious of your path and the choices that lead down it.

Affirmations 201-300

201) I am a strong and independent man.

202) I am becoming healthier every day.

203) I can always find time for myself.

204) I deserve all of the good in life.

205) I deserve to be happy and healthy.

206) I have the power to shape my life.

207) I make a difference in this world.

208) I take control of every situation.

209) I'm more awesome than ever before.

210) My confidence is my secret weapon.

211) My future is bright and beautiful.

212) My mind is free of fear and doubt.

213) My shoulders are broad and strong.

214) This will be my greatest year yet.

215) I am a man of power and prosperity.

216) I am a positive, successful person.

217) I am a very happy and grateful man.

218) I am so grateful to be alive today.

219) I am strong, confident and focused.

220) I am taking my life back right now.

221) I am the master of my own emotions.

222) I am the owner of my own happiness.

223) I am worthy of receiving abundance.

224) I can do anything I set my mind to.

225) I deserve great success in my life.

226) I have the power to change my life.

227) I know a lot about a lot of things.

228) I love what I do, and I do it well.

229) I will not give up on my potential.

230) I'm constantly growing as a person.

231) My attitude determines my altitude.

232) My confidence is growing every day.

233) My life is fun, happy, and healthy.

234) My mind is calm and peaceful today.

235) My mind is powerful and commanding.

236) My past does not dictate my future.

237) Patience is one of my best virtues.

238) Success follows me everywhere I go.

239) The more I work, the luckier I get.

240) The present moment is all there is.

241) I can laugh at life's little jokes.

242) All of life's answers are within me.

243) Every moment is full of opportunity.

244) I am a man of leadership and vision.

245) I am a man of strength and vitality.

246) I am strong, masculine and powerful.

247) I am thankful for what I have today.

248) I am the master of my body and mind.

249) I deserve to be celebrated every day.

250) I respect myself and others can too.

251) If other people can do it, so can I.

252) Laughter is truly the best medicine.

253) My life may not be perfect but I am.

254) My success follows me wherever I go.

255) My voice is sexier than ever before.

256) The world loves me as I love myself.

257) This day is going to be a great day.

258) All good things come to me right now.

259) All of my actions are guided by love.

260) All that is in my path shall be mine.

261) Everything is unfolding as it should.

262) I am committed to being my best self.

263) I am constantly learning and growing.

264) I am dedicated to lifelong learning.

265) I am in charge of my current reality.

266) I am self-confident and self-assured.

267) I am strong, confident, and powerful.

268) I believe in myself and my abilities.

269) I have the power to make today great.

270) I love to learn new things every day.

271) I see everyone as beautiful and kind.

272) If opportunity doesn't knock, I will.

273) My confidence is at an all-time high.

274) My days are filled with appreciation.

275) My mind is clear and calm, right now.

276) My mind is clear; my heart is strong.

277) People are naturally attracted to me.

278) Success is drawn to me like a magnet.

279) The harder I work, the luckier I get.

280) What's meant for me won't pass me by.

281) Winning is a natural part of my life.

282) I am a successful and abundant person.

283) All good things are flowing to me now.

284) Every moment is a chance to be strong.

285) Everything about me oozes masculinity.

286) Great opportunities are headed my way.

287) I am confident, capable and competent.

288) I am embracing my masculine sexuality.

289) I am filled with strength and courage.

290) I am grateful for all of life's gifts.

291) I am more than what they say about me.

292) I am strong in mind, body, and spirit.

293) I deserve love, respect and happiness.

294) I enjoy my work and always do my best.

295) I put all my energy behind what I say.

296) Life gets better and better every day.

297) My favorite person of all time is me.

298) My heart is open and full of love now.

299) My mind is filled with creative ideas.

300) My thoughts are clear and focused now.

04

Lesson IV. Diligence

The warrior in you isn't afraid of hard work - because he knows that doing nothing is harder than anything else. He has no time or patience for laziness and will never feel sorry for himself, even when the odds are against him.

Challenge: Improve your posture

Keep an upright posture for the whole day and no matter what you are doing; walking, taking a shower or even sitting. Stand up straight with your shoulders back, chin parallel to the ground and feet hip-width apart.

Take note of how this simple change in posture can affect your whole day. You'll feel more confident about yourself because you are holding yourself in a more powerful position.

Doing this for 30 days straight will help you develop better posture, which will naturally lead to greater confidence.

When you're walking, picture yourself wearing a cape that's tugging your shoulder back. This will help you keep a straight posture and feel more powerful.

Affirmations 301-400

301) Taking risks is what leads to success.

302) My work today will be a great success.

303) Today I feel light, free and at peace.

304) Today is the day to make things right.

305) When opportunities arise, I take them.

306) Every day I find a new way to have fun.

307) Every day, my inner core gets stronger.

308) Every day is a day to try something new.

309) I am a man of abundance and prosperity.

310) I am a man who is incredibly confident.

311) I am becoming more confident every day.

312) I am committed to finding my own truth.

313) I am the architect of my own happiness.

314) I deserve to be incredibly happy today.

315) I have the power to change my thoughts.

316) I now believe in my ability to succeed.

317) I stay calm and focused under pressure.

318) Life just gets better every single day.

319) My body is healthy, strong and natural.

320) My life is the best movie in the world.

321) My mind is open, receptive and relaxed.

322) My sexual energy is immense and strong.

323) New doors are opening for me every day.

324) People are drawn to my positive energy.

325) People view me as a pillar of strength.

326) Success is a process of self-discovery.

327) The more I learn, the smarter I become.

328) The more I struggle, the stronger I am.

329) Today holds great possibilities for me.

330) Today I will live life on my own terms.

331) Today is going to be the best day ever.

332) Women admire my confidence and courage.

333) Every breath I take, I take in strength.

334) I acknowledge all of my successes today.

335) I am a man of iron discipline and focus.

336) I am a man of strength and fear nothing.

337) I am always open to learning new things.

338) I am at peace with the world and myself.

339) I am filled with happy, joyous thoughts.

340) I am passionate about living positively.

341) I am willing to learn what I don't know.

342) I am willing to stretch myself and grow.

343) I appreciate all that life has to offer.

344) I deserve to live the life of my dreams.

345) I deserve to relax and have lots of fun.

346) I give and receive love unconditionally.

347) I release the past and seize the future.

348) I will always be the best that I can be.

349) Life is better when lived at full speed.

350) My body is built for pleasure, not pain.

351) My heart is full of love and compassion.

352) My life is magical and filled with ease.

353) My mind is still and focused on success.

354) My power is unbreakable and unstoppable.

355) No one can resist my charm and charisma.

356) Others see my true leadership abilities.

357) The answers I need are always within me.

358) There is nothing that I cannot do today.

359) Today I know who I am and I like myself.

360) Today is the beginning of something big.

361) All of my goals are well within my reach.

362) Each new day becomes perfect as it comes.

363) Every day my life gets better and better.

364) Everything always works out for the best.

365) I am at peace with where I am in my life.

366) I am confident in who I am and I like it.

367) I am in control of my moods and emotions.

368) I am more than good enough for the world.

369) I am not small because my dreams are big.

370) I am surrounded by loving, caring people.

371) I am unstoppable and nothing can stop me.

372) I can do anything if I believe in myself.

373) I can do anything if I put my mind to it.

374) I deserve all the good life has to offer.

375) I deserve to be loved and that is a fact.

376) I focus on what is going well in my life.

377) I see myself as a manly, masculine being.

378) I use my power to help myself and others.

379) If I stay positive, the sky is the limit.

380) Life is working out for me in every area.

381) My body is beautiful, healthy and strong.

382) My body is rejuvenating itself every day.

383) My dreams are reality today and every day.

384) My mind is calm and at peace with itself.

385) My mind is sharp and my body is powerful.

386) Today I am going to take a leap of faith.

387) Today is full of wonderful possibilities.

388) Today will be great because I make it so.

389) Today, life is full of peace and harmony.

390) A thankful attitude will produce abundance.

391) Every day, I become more and more awesome.

392) I always choose happiness over negativity.

393) I am a dragon disguised in a sheep's skin.

394) I am a man of power, never knowing defeat.

395) I am a man who knows how to use his words.

396) I am enjoying life to the full, right now.

397) I am not perfect, but I always do my best.

398) I am the master of my mind, not its slave.

399) I am worthy of receiving the best in life.

400) I believe in myself and everyone knows it.

05

Lesson V. Confidence

The warrior in you is confident - because he knows that feeling fear means feeling vulnerable. He will never give in to his fears; he has the strength, the courage and the determination to overcome them.

Challenge: Do something painful

Doing something that scares you every day for a week helps to take your self-esteem and emotional well-being to the next level. Doing this each day for even just 5 minutes is enough to create an aura of confidence around you, which will help attract more confident people into your life.

Look at everything that makes you feel uneasy. Make a list of all of these items. These can be anything from public speaking, dancing in front of people, striking up conversations with strangers or asking that cute person out for coffee.

Now, think about how you could overcome these fears. You might start small by only doing the thing that makes you just a little uneasy and build up your confidence, then eventually work your way up to something more challenging.

For example, if you are afraid of dancing in front of people, start by going to a dance class until you build up the courage to go invite your friends out with you and surprise them without warning by busting out an amazing dance move.

You may begin by saying hello to some strangers while on your way somewhere or at an event if you are scared of interacting with other people. It's not necessary to begin any conversations with them. Then, once you've mastered that, attempt to start a conversation with someone you don't know.

By overcoming these small fears that hold you back from experiencing life, your confidence will grow exponentially. The majority of the concerns you imagined would happen will not occur. Knowing that you can do anything no matter what scares you is a sign of pure mental fortitude.

Affirmations 401-500

401) I command respect from everyone around me.

402) I deserve the best that life has to offer.

403) I deserve to relax and enjoy myself today.

404) I focus my energy on making great choices.

405) I forgive myself for all my past mistakes.

406) I refuse to let anyone limit my potential.

407) I see opportunity everywhere I look today.

408) My body works efficiently and effectively.

409) My voice is rich, captivating and sensual.

410) My work time is full of joy and happiness.

411) My worth increases with every passing day.

412) Nothing can stop me now; I am unstoppable.

413) Other people look up to me for leadership.

414) The only thing that limits me, is my mind.

415) Today, I am living in harmony with nature.

416) I am one of life's natural success stories.

417) I am the lord and master of my own destiny.

418) Everything in my life happens for a reason.

419) I always maintain composure under pressure.

420) I am a winner and my success is inevitable.

421) I am an interesting and fascinating person.

422) I am ready for whatever comes my way today.

423) I deserve all the wonderful things in life.

424) I deserve to be healthy, wealthy and happy.

425) I have power over my thoughts and feelings.

426) I love and accept myself just the way I am.

427) I release others' control over my life now.

428) I trust myself to make the right decisions.

429) Life is waiting on me so get out of my way.

430) My creativity is expressed through my work.

431) My mind is calm and at peace with serenity.

432) My mind is free from worry, doubt and fear.

433) My voice is deep, powerful, and commanding.

434) Today is all about me because it is my day.

435) When I let go of my past, I release regret.

436) All of my needs are met in this very moment.

437) All those who truly love me surround me now.

438) I allow success to flow easily into my life.

439) I am a magnet. I attract success and wealth.

440) I am a man that is calm, cool and collected.

441) I am living life for myself and no one else.

442) I am smart enough, and I am talented enough.

443) I have everything that I need within myself.

444) I know how to make something out of nothing.

445) I love how much stronger my body is getting.

446) I refuse to be a victim of my circumstances.

447) Life gives me pleasure. I give life meaning.

448) Life loves me. All is going well for me now.

449) My body is becoming healthy and strong.

450) My deep voice commands everyone's attention.

451) My mind is always open to new possibilities.

452) My mind is unstoppable and I am unstoppable.

453) No one can resist me when I put on my charm.

454) Success flows to me easily and effortlessly.

455) The more I learn, the more wisdom I acquire.

456) The more success I create, the better life gets.

457) Today I make a positive impact on the world.

458) Today I will accomplish more than yesterday.

459) Today is my day, and I will make it amazing.

460) All negative people are a drain on my energy.

461) All successful people make money their slave.

462) As I learn more, I realize how little I know.

463) Every day, I become more confident in myself.

464) I always bring positive energy into the room.

465) I am a great communicator and problem solver.

466) I am a man of my word; I am honest and loyal.

467) I am a powerful creator of money and success.

468) I am filled with gratitude for my life today.

469) I can achieve anything that I set my mind to.

470) I can find a way to get what I need and want.

471) I choose to create success, not just seek it.

472) I deserve to be happy and laughing right now.

473) I deserve to be wealthy, and I accept it now.

474) I deserve to live a happy and fulfilled life.

475) I go after what I want in life, and I get it.

476) I love who I am and who I have yet to become.

477) I lovingly release all negative ties that bind me now.

478) I will never stop improving my mind and body.

479) I will not let my past define who I am today.

480) Life is beautiful so I will always be humble.

481) My future is filled with unlimited potential.

482) My intuition helps guide me towards my goals.

483) My mind is calm no matter what the situation.

484) Now is a time to celebrate how far I've come.

485) Success is not a destination, it's a journey.

486) The more I try, the better my results become.

487) What I learn today is important to my future.

488) Women love me when I am assertive and strong.

489) A day where nothing gets done is a day wasted.

490) Each day, my mind becomes clearer and clearer.

491) I always attract positive energy into my life.

492) I am a magnet to all the opportunities I need.

493) I am a man who will not be denied his success.

494) I am a man with strength, passion, and energy.

495) I am a success magnet. Success is drawn to me.

496) I am always improving myself at whatever I do.

497) I am deeply interested in the world around me.

498) I am drawn to success as if by magnetic force.

499) I am good with money, and money is good to me.

500) I am growing in strength and wisdom every day.

06

Lesson VI. Responsibility

The warrior in you is a good man - because he takes responsibility for his actions and never makes excuses for them. He knows that being true to yourself means being true to other people as well, and treats all people that deserve it with kindness and respect.

Challenge: Find out what you are good at

Knowing what you are actually good at can be a challenge. To help you identify this, ask yourself what you are proud of having achieved in the past. When was the last time that something amazing happened to you?

At first this might be difficult because we tend to focus on our failures rather than our successes. By looking at these things and celebrating them, you will begin to realize what you are actually good at and proud of.

Keeping track of everything that made you feel proud will help you see what you are actually good at. Be honest with yourself and write down everything, no matter how small or silly it may seem.

Once you've identified what your best attributes are, you should try to improve these even more. A standstill is, in fact, a type of declination that causes you to feel uninspired. Make sure to grow as a person by considering your own assets.

Affirmations 501-600

501) I am in charge of every situation that arises.

502) I am more than enough, just the way that I am.

503) I am open to the flow of abundance in my life.

504) I am strong, confident, capable, and powerful.

505) I am unique and my life is full of excitement.

506) I can accomplish anything I set my mind to do.

507) I can always find time to take care of myself.

508) I deserve to be healthy, happy and prosperous.

509) I deserve to be successful, happy and healthy.

510) I deserve to have all the good things in life.

511) I follow through with everything that I start.

512) I really know how to get the good out of life.

513) I take action because that is what winners do.

514) Infinite opportunities are now flowing my way.

515) It's time to go out there and get what's mine.

516) Life is too short to waste being sad or angry.

517) My body functions at its very best, right now.

518) My body is healthy, strong and full of energy.

519) My business is growing at an exponential rate.

520) My family and friends love me unconditionally.

521) My happiness level is off the chart right now.

522) My mind cannot be penetrated by doubt or fear.

523) My mind is sharp, focused, and full of energy.

524) My mind, body and soul are strong and healthy.

525) People love me for being me, not someone else.

526) People respect me the more masculine I become.

527) People trust me because I am a man of my word.

528) Successful, powerful and abundant - that's me.

529) The best is yet to come, and it's coming soon.

530) The sun always rises to bring new opportunity.

531) The world is mine because I refuse to give up.

532) There is nothing holding me back from success.

533) Today, I take a stand against all of my fears.

534) As a man, I can endure all things and be happy.

535) Every day is filled with endless possibilities.

536) Every day, I find time to relax and enjoy life.

537) Every time I fall, I get stronger and stronger.

538) Everything good comes from within me right now.

539) I am grateful for who I am and all that I have.

540) I am greater than what my past can ever define.

541) I am powerful and in control of my own reality.

542) I am thankful for all of my friends and family.

543) I am worthy of living a happy and wealthy life.

544) I can accomplish anything that I set out to do.

545) I can choose love and happiness no matter what.

546) I focus on my goals and crush them immediately.

547) I give myself permission to be happy right now.

548) I give myself permission to look awesome today.

549) I have everything I need to be happy right now.

550) I only attract the best into my life right now.

551) I only do the best I can, and then I let it go.

552) I will not give up because I know I am special.

553) It's never too late for me to follow my dreams.

554) Life is easier when you have faith in yourself.

555) Life will not be easy, but it will be worth it.

556) Money comes to me easily and effortlessly, now.

557) My inner strength motivates me towards success.

558) My life is full of variety, fun, and adventure.

559) My life purpose is to be the best man possible.

560) My mind is filled with peace and clarity today.

561) My positive thoughts create a positive reality.

562) My testosterone levels are optimal and healthy.

563) My thoughts are focused, positive and powerful.

564) People who love me, know how to value my worth.

565) The energy of my mind and body knows no limits.

566) The more I relax, the better things get for me.

567) The sexual energy within me has been unleashed.

568) The wisdom of life is flowing through me today.

569) Today I embrace change, and I love the journey.

570) Today, I will do one thing that makes me happy.

571) Today, life gives back all that I've given out.

572) When I have nothing, is when my success begins.

573) Each day I change the way I think, feel and act.

574) Every day brings a new chance for me to succeed.

575) Every day is a new opportunity to be successful.

576) Everything that has happened is for my own good.

577) I am a man of greatness so anything is possible.

578) I am a man that is deeply fulfilled by his work.

579) I am an unstoppable juggernaut of human success.

580) I am at peace with myself, others and the world.

581) I am becoming more and more patient with myself.

582) I am courageous to take action despite my fears.

583) I am mentally invincible and will never give up.

584) I am ready for anything that comes my way today.

585) I attract abundance and success everywhere I go.

586) I channel masculinity through my body every day.

587) I choose to live life happy and free from worry.

588) I choose to see the good in people, not the bad.

589) I deserve the best in life, and I accept it now.

590) I embrace all opportunities to grow and prosper.

591) I have everything I need to be successful today.

592) I love to learn about the world of spirituality.

593) I make time for the important things in my life.

594) I'm proud of who I am and not afraid to show it.

595) I'm stronger than any problem that comes my way.

596) My income is increasing tremendously, right now.

597) No one can break me because I am already broken.

598) Successful people are not afraid of the word no.

599) Successful people help me become successful too.

600) The world rewards me for all of my hard work.

07

Lesson VII. Perseverance

The warrior in you refuses to give up - not on his family, his business or anything that's important to him. He knows that every problem has a solution and he will do whatever it takes to find out what it is.

Challenge: Cultivate a positive outlook on life

Having a positive outlook on life is crucial to having confidence. A negative mind will tear you down, sap your motivation and sap your confidence. A positive mind will help you achieve new goals, become more successful and feel more confident than ever before.

With all the challenges that life throws at us, it's important that we stay on top of them all. We need to cultivate a positive outlook on life that will help us face any challenge.

The way you look at something is how you shape the outcome of it. If you're looking at challenges in your life with optimism, they become easier to overcome and lead to greater success.

To start, try to see the good in every challenge you face. If there wasn't a challenge, you wouldn't have had the opportunity to grow. Think of every obstacle as something that will inevitably help you become better at life and make your path more interesting. Every success has challenges before it, so embrace them with open arms because they're what makes you stronger.

Every time something negative happens in your day, look at the bright side of it. The bad stuff in life is going to happen, but say "I'm going to make this work for me" instead of "this sucks". Even something as simple as that can change your outlook on life and help you achieve whatever makes you happy.

Affirmations 601-700

601) Today is filled with wonders beyond imagination.

602) Something good always comes out of something bad.

603) Do it today because tomorrow is never guaranteed.

604) Every day I gain more confidence and self-esteem.

605) I always attract the perfect opportunities to me.

606) I am a man who will not give up on his potential.

607) I am an unstoppable force that cannot be stopped.

608) I am open to all the good that life has to offer.

609) I am strong, confident, and secure in my manhood.

610) I am the chosen one and my success is inevitable.

611) I can achieve anything if I have faith in myself.

612) I can do anything if I stick with it long enough.

613) I give myself permission to relax and enjoy life.

614) I happily provide value for other people's lives.

615) I have all the potential, just believe in myself.

616) I have everything that it takes to be successful.

617) I lift heavier weights every time that I work out.

618) I welcome change as a challenge, not as a threat.

619) It doesn't matter what other people think or say.

620) Money flows to me freely, abundantly, and easily.

621) My body is lean, hard, sexy, strong and youthful.

622) My heart pumps pure awesomeness through my veins.

623) My level of calmness under pressure is inspiring.

624) My mind is filled with positive energy right now.

625) My mind is focused on peace and prosperity today.

626) My mind is full of confidence and self-assurance.

627) My mind is sharp, focused, and extremely capable.

628) My positive thoughts are taking shape in reality.

629) No matter how tough the workout, I never give up.

630) Obstacles cannot stop me from achieving my goals.

631) The more I give, the more I am capable of giving.

632) The more obstacles I face, the stronger I become.

633) Today I choose to be happy, no matter how I feel.

634) Today I will take a step in a positive direction.

635) Today, I am more masculine than I have ever been.

636) Women are attracted to me because I am confident.

637) All of my relationships are healthy and rewarding.

638) Breathing in positivity; breathing out negativity.

639) Doing my best is getting me to where I want to be.

640) Even when times are tough, there is always hope.

641) Every day brings me closer to achieving my dreams.

642) Every day I learn something that makes me smarter.

643) I am a magnet for prosperity and wealth right now.

644) I am a rock against which the waves of life crash.

645) I am able to accomplish anything I put my mind to.

646) I am at peace with myself and the world around me.

647) I am calm, relaxed, and comfortable with who I am.

648) I am exactly where I am supposed to be in my life.

649) I am strong, and my strength comes from within me.

650) I attract only good things into my life right now.

651) I can do anything, as long as I believe in myself.

652) I can let go of anything that no longer serves me.

653) I deserve all of the good things that come my way.

654) I deserve all the wealth and riches of this world.

655) I deserve success just as much as the next person.

656) I deserve to be happy, no matter what anyone says.

657) I have strength inside of me that no one else has.

658) I have the power to change my life for the better.

659) I possess within me an unlimited amount of energy.

660) My attitude is infectious. People are drawn to me.

661) My body works better when I give it what it needs.

662) My heart is pure, so I am able to see clearly now.

663) My success is inevitable because I am unstoppable.

664) My success is inevitable because I refuse to quit.

665) No one can take away my confidence and self-worth.

666) People are drawn to me; they want to be my friend.

667) People are drawn to my positive energy, right now.

668) People love seeing an underdog rise up to the top.

669) Success is my duty, obligation and responsibility.

670) The law of attraction is working for me right now.

671) The more that I learn, the better my life becomes.

672) There are too many people depending on me to quit.

673) This moment is a gift. I treasure it. I love it.

674) When I feel sorry for myself, it's just self-pity.

675) With every breath I take, new potential awaits me.

676) The best is yet to come. Today is my new beginning.

677) All good things come to me easily and effortlessly.

678) All of my dreams are coming true one day at a time.

679) All of my dreams are coming true, little by little.

680) Each day I grow in strength, knowledge, and wisdom.

681) Each day that passes brings me closer to my dreams.

682) Every day is a chance to do something that matters.

683) I am a magnet for success and prosperity right now.

684) I am always getting better at everything that I do.

685) I am grateful for the challenges that I learn from.

686) I am stronger than any challenge that comes my way.

687) I am surrounded by people that love and support me.

688) I choose to make every day the best day of my life.

689) I deserve all the abundance that life has to offer.

690) I have a good life, and that is why I am a success.

691) I have my entire life to be the best that I can be.

692) I have unlimited potential to make myself stronger.

693) I live with confidence because I stand by who I am.

694) I love myself and everyone in my life loves me too.

695) I will invite success into my life and not failure.

696) It takes a lot of courage to take a chance in life.

697) My imagination is my preview of coming attractions.

698) My income will increase at a steady pace this year.

699) No one can push me down because I'm already on top.

700) People are friendly, life is full of opportunities.

08

Lesson VIII. Values

The warrior in you never betrays his values - even when they are inconvenient or make others uncomfortable. He never sacrifices his principles for the sake of expediency or feigns piety in order to make an impression, no matter how grave the consequences.

Challenge: Learn Gratitude

Practice gratitude for all the good in your life, big and small. Being grateful helps you to be more conscious and aware of all that is good in yourself and your environment. This leads to a positive mindset, which helps you attract more positivity into your life.

To start, write down five things that you are grateful for today. As time goes on, challenge yourself to find more meaningful things to be grateful for as you go through your day.

Practice gratitude at least once every day. Remember that the smallest events in our lives count as opportunities to practice gratitude. From the delicious food you eat, to your favorite movie or book, to the beautiful person on your arm, there is everything in life to be grateful for.

As you begin to point out all of these positive things to yourself, you will notice a shift in your attitude.

Affirmations 701-800

701) The future of my family depends on what I do today.

702) The more I help others, the better my life becomes.

703) The stronger I become; the less people can hurt me.

704) When I help others, life becomes easier for me too.

705) Each morning, I grow more than I did the day before.

706) Every day I grow stronger in body, mind, and spirit.

707) Every day, I am becoming the best version of myself.

708) Every moment of every day is filled with positivity.

709) I always have plenty, and I give without hesitation.

710) I am a champion of life; I deserve the best in life.

711) I am a man of action, believing in my own abilities.

712) I am a man who leads, inspires and motivates others.

713) I am filled with confidence and free from all doubt.

714) I am getting better every day with every experience.

715) I am so excited to see what this year brings for me.

716) I enjoy being healthy and I am grateful for my body.

717) I have a healthy relationship with food and my body.

718) I have what it takes to turn my dreams into reality.

719) I release all worries and experience only peace now.

720) I will choose happiness over fear, every single day.

721) I will have a better day today than I did yesterday.

722) I will never judge others because it's not worth it.

723) My actions inspire others to follow in my footsteps.

724) My days are filled with joy, laughter and happiness.

725) My discipline is the subject of envy and admiration.

726) My lessons are clear, simple and easy to understand.

727) My mind is always calm no matter what the situation.

728) No one can push me down because I am already on top.

729) No one, and nothing can stop me from being who I am.

730) People are naturally attracted to my inner-strength.

731) Success comes easily because my mind is unstoppable.

732) The harder I work; the luckier life will get for me.

733) The more I relax, the better everything gets for me.

734) The more relaxed I am, the better things get for me.

735) Today is a new beginning where anything is possible.

736) Today is the day I choose to succeed so bring it on.

737) Today, and every day, life brings me many blessings.

738) The faster I achieve my goals, the happier I become.

739) A life without challenges is a life not worth living.

740) Every day I learn something new that makes me better.

741) Every day, I become more masculine and more of a man.

742) Every day, I become more successful in all that I do.

743) I am a protector and a provider for those who I love.

744) I am becoming more confident in everything that I do.

745) I deserve to relax and enjoy life's little pleasures.

746) I make wise decisions each day that affect my future.

747) I release my past and live in the present moment now.

748) I will never settle for less because I know my worth.

749) I'm going to have the best day of my life. Everyday.

750) In every challenge I see an opportunity for strength.

751) It's okay to be afraid, but I must do my best anyway.

752) Money and success come to me easily and effortlessly.

753) My happiness comes from what I give, not what I take.

754) My mind is powerful, confident, sharp and commanding.

755) My past failure does not define who I am as a person.

756) My positive thoughts create healthy new habits in me.

757) My voice is powerful, commanding, confident and sexy.

758) My work is filled with abundance, joy and prosperity.

759) Nothing holds me back from my full potential in life.

760) Now is my time. Today is the perfect day to be alive.

761) People are not shy to ask for help; I give it freely.

762) Successful people are grateful, generous and helpful.

763) The moment is always ripe for change and improvement.

764) The more fun I have today, the better my day will be.

765) The more I do for others, the better my life becomes.

766) The power of my mind expands exponentially every day.

767) The world around me is a reflection of my inner self.

768) Today is my day so whatever happens, it is my choice.

769) Today will bring another opportunity for me to excel.

770) Today, and every day, I expect good things to happen.

771) Life loves me and showers me with abundance right now.

772) People respect me and they admire me at the same time.

773) All of my relationships are based on love and support.

774) All of the best things are ahead of me, not behind me.

775) At this very moment, life is working perfectly for me.

776) Every day is another opportunity to make a difference.

777) I always know what is most important for me right now.

778) I am a man of my word and I will always do what I say.

779) I am a man of peace and do not fight without the need.

780) I am a warrior who will fight for greatness every day.

781) I am confident in my own unique talents and abilities.

782) I am going to be happy right now because I deserve it.

783) I am surrounded by loving supportive people right now.

784) I am unstoppable and there is no one that can stop me.

785) I choose to love myself today, just as I am right now.

786) I do not have to be perfect because nobody is perfect.

787) I have the best friends and family in the whole world.

788) Life is so much better when you're positive and happy.

789) My attitude is always positive no matter what happens.

790) My goals flow to me now as I am ready to achieve them.

791) My masculinity shines through in everything that I do.

792) My mind is filled with ideas, inspiration, and vision.

793) My mindset controls my life, not the other way around.

794) My success starts today and it is going to be amazing.

795) People can't hurt me anymore because I respect myself.

796) Success is my calling in life so I will be successful.

797) Successful people plan their work and work their plan.

798) The more I give, the better things come back to me.

799) The more things I have to do, the better my life gets.

800) You will never find a man as confident and sexy as me.

09

Lesson IX. Experience

The warrior in you is always learning - because he knows that there will always be something that he doesn't know and that it's important to be open to new ideas.

Challenge: Get out of your comfort zone

Get out of your comfort zone to become more comfortable with yourself and ultimately gain confidence

The ultimate goal of everything we do, whether it's a new career path, starting a family or moving to another country, is to feel completely comfortable and confident in our decision. Getting out of your comfort zone will take you closer to this feeling of confidence and self-comfort.

Since most of us spend most of our days in our comfort zones, we don't push ourselves out of them very often. This lack of discomfort is unnatural and unhealthy for the mind because it stagnates your ability to grow.

Here's one challenge that will help you get out: Try a new activity that you have been wanting to do for a while. It doesn't matter how challenging it is, just push yourself out of your comfort zone and remember that the only way to feel more comfortable with yourself is by getting uncomfortable.

You will notice that getting out of your comfort zone will lead to more opportunities and growth. This is because once you get past the initial fear, you are able to accomplish things that you never thought yourself capable of doing.

Affirmations 801-900

801) All of the good that is coming into my life, right now.

802) Every problem comes with a solution, so I must find it.

803) I am grateful for the lessons that I have gained today.

804) I am the head of my home. I am the leader of my family.

805) I command myself to relax and enjoy this beautiful day.

806) I command total financial success for myself right now.

807) I feel confident speaking in front of groups of people.

808) I have everything that I need to be successful in life.

809) I have unlimited potential to be the best man possible.

810) I owe it to myself to become as successful as possible.

811) I refuse to let my fears stop me from being successful.

812) I will let my mistakes serve as their own lesson to me.

813) If you believe in yourself, you will do amazing things.

814) It's okay if I don't get everything right all the time.

815) My future is filled with happiness, joy and prosperity.

816) My inner vision is always clearer than my outer vision.

817) My masculine energy is strong but also kind and loving.

818) No matter how bad things seem, the best is yet to come.

819) No matter how difficult the challenge, I never give up.

820) No one can push me around because I live in the moment.

821) Obstacles are stepping stones that guide me to success.

822) The harder the conflict, the more glorious the triumph.

823) The only thing standing between me and success is fear.

824) The world is a place of wonder, beauty, and excitement.

825) Today I will be the most confident person in the world.

826) Opportunity is all around me, waiting to be seen by me.

827) Every day I become more disciplined than the day before.

828) Every day is a new beginning and an opportunity to grow.

829) Every day is a new beginning with endless possibilities.

830) Every day that goes by I become better at whatever I do.

831) Every day, I become more powerful than the previous day.

832) I am a man of my word and I know the value of hard work.

833) I am a man who speaks with power, precision and passion.

834) I am capable of so much more than I've done in the past.

835) I am inspired to accomplish great things today.

836) I am feeling better and better with each passing moment.

837) I am getting stronger and better with every passing day.

838) I am not afraid to take risks, only rewards interest me.

839) I am strong enough to handle anything life throws at me.

840) I deserve to live the life of my dreams and I do so now.

841) I feel powerful when walking into a room full of people.

842) I give myself permission to be powerful and unstoppable.

843) I have everything I need in order to be happy right now.

844) I have unlimited potential to continue growing as a man.

845) I refuse to let anyone tell me what to do or how to act.

846) I think thoughts that are positive and empowering to me.

847) It's okay to have a bad day, as long as I don't give up.

848) My body is capable of incredible strength and endurance.

849) My clarity is powerful; it brings me closer to my goals.

850) My mistakes are not failures but rather lessons learned.

851) The more that I help others, the better my life will be.

852) The only thing that is constant in this world is change.

853) The strength of my body lies in the strength of my mind.

854) The world is full of opportunities for me to succeed in.

855) The world is my playground where I can achieve anything.

856) Today I will let go of my regret and embrace the future.

857) Today is all about finding peace and balance in my life.

858) Right in this second, life is working out perfectly for me.

859) All of my productive time this day is spent making money.

860) All things are achievable through persistence and effort.

861) As soon as one project is complete, I will begin another.

862) Every day is a gift because it's another day to be happy.

863) Every day, I become more determined to achieve my dreams.

864) Every day, I make positive choices that are right for me.

865) Everything I need to be happy is coming my way right now.

866) I am a fast learner and quick to adapt to new situations.

867) I am a force to be reckoned with and nothing can stop me.

868) I am a man of honor and dignity, willing to serve others.

869) I am a strong leader who others look up to for direction.

870) I am always looking for new and interesting things to do.

871) I am full of life and energy, ready to conquer the world.

872) I am surrounded by inspiration from all corners of the world.

873) I am the star in this movie called life, so I must shine.

874) I am very intuitive. I trust my feelings and act on them.

875) I can accomplish anything as long as I believe in myself.

876) I deserve the best in life because I work hard to get it.

877) I do not compete with others; I only compete with myself.

878) I follow my heart's guidance with courage and conviction.

879) I possess a magnetic personality that draws people to me.

880) I will keep going until everything in my life is perfect.

881) I will not let my fears keep me from achieving greatness.

882) I'm going to take all the opportunities that I can today.

883) Life is easy when you know who you are and what you want.

884) My body is my vehicle towards success; I take care of it.

885) My heart is open and full of love towards everyone today.

886) My past does not dictate my future because I am a winner.

887) No one has power over me unless I permit them to have it.

888) No one has the ability to make my choices for me anymore.

889) Success is not beyond my reach; it's mine for the taking.

890) The more relaxed I become, the easier I can breathe.

891) Wealth and abundance are flowing into my life, right now.

892) I will not give up on what I want because it will be mine.

893) My business will be booming. Money comes easily to me now.

894) As I improve myself, everything around me gets better too.

895) Discipline is the bridge between goals and accomplishment.

896) Excuses are a temporary thing but greatness lasts forever.

897) I allow life to flow through me easily, I don't resist it.

898) I am a man of virtue; my words are truthful and uplifting.

899) I am a man who is in charge of his life and circumstances.

900) I am the author of my life. And it's a good story so far.

10

Lesson X. Excuses

The warrior in you doesn't make excuses - for things over which he has no control. He knows the only thing he can really change is himself, so he doesn't try to be something he's not.

Challenge: Take responsibility

Taking responsibility for your actions will help you become more confident because it forces you to appreciate your surroundings.

Most people are quick to blame others for their problems, but this can cause a lot of negativities in your life. When you always blame other people or factors that are out of your control for the things that go wrong, you lose sight of the things that you could have done to prevent it.

We need to take responsibility for our actions and see the ways we can improve them in order to move forward with confidence. Instead of blaming others, find out where your paths split and recognize if the mistake was actually yours to begin with. This will help you become more confident because you'll become more aware of your actions and decisions. When you become more aware, you'll be able to make better choices that lead to a better outcome – whether it's overcoming a challenge or meeting a goal.

To start, make a list of all the things that went wrong throughout your last week. This doesn't necessarily mean horrible things like getting arrested, but also simple mistakes like being late for work. If you're having trouble remembering them, remind yourself to look at your phone and jot down an event each time it happens.

Once you have your list, go over it and take note of the situations that you could've avoided. Look back and check if it was your behavior that had a part in it or if it was out of your control. If you did have a part in it which is often the case, try to think about what you could have done better to improve or prevent the situation.

To be absolutely clear, this is not about publicly taking the blame for something, but rather about learning from your errors. You'll always make mistakes throughout your life, but they're not good learning opportunities if you don't take responsibility for them.

After you finish your list, make a plan of action for how you can avoid these mistakes in the future. There's always something we can improve in our lives.

Affirmations 901-1000

901) I appreciate my body for all that it does for me each day.

902) I can do anything as long as I believe that it's possible.

903) I have many interests and hobbies to keep my mind engaged.

904) I look for opportunities in everything that happens to me.

905) I love to learn new things about my body, mind and spirit.

906) I stay motivated by thoughts of my superior muscle growth.

907) I treat myself with respect and dignity as a powerful man.

908) I will give 100% today because that is what life deserves.

909) I will let my optimism shine for everyone around me today.

910) I will never give up on myself because my dreams are real.

911) I've managed to survive so far, and today is no exception.

912) Life has given me a precious gift in the form of this day.

913) Life is taking care of me in every way possible right now.

914) My body is strong and healthy and works just as it should.

915) My eyes are open and perceive the light of love around me.

916) My life has purpose because my thoughts create my reality.

917) My physical body is becoming more masculine by the second.

918) My physical strength is only matched by my inner strength.

919) People notice my strong physique and strong body language.

920) The more grateful I am, the more abundant my life becomes.

921) The real power lies within me, not in the problems I face.

922) The world is always changing; I am able to change with it.

923) Today is a new beginning, starting my life all over again.

924) Today is the day to be positive; there is no other choice.

925) What others say and think about me is none of my business.

926) When I think of something positive, I speak it into being.

927) Women love me for my strength. Women love me for my power.

928) As far as I am concerned, today is the best day of my life.

929) Every day is a new beginning and not the end of my success.

930) Every exercise that I do builds strength every single time.

931) Fear is not real, it's just an illusion created in my mind.

932) I am a magnet of success; I attract it without even trying.

933) I am a man of honor and keep my word to those I care about.

934) I am a work of art and my masterpiece is who I am becoming.

935) I am an example for other people, so I must always do good.

936) I am at peace with who I am and my life is filled with joy.

937) I am becoming more loving with myself and others every day.

938) I am the future and everyone else better get out of my way.

939) I believe in my heart that everything happens for a reason.

940) I deserve all of the good things that are coming to me now.

941) I give thanks for all the good that is coming into my life.

942) I have everything I need to enjoy the present moment fully.

943) I have the power to achieve anything that I set my mind to.

944) I live in the present where I am safe, cared for and loved.

945) I will not let my past hold me back from being great today.

946) I will use my masculine energy to create a healthier world.

947) It's okay to fall down, because I always get back up again.

948) Life is easier when you know who you are and what you want.

949) My biggest goal is well on its way to completion right now.

950) My future looks bright surrounded by so many loving people.

951) My income is growing at an ideal rate for me and my family.

952) My mind is sharp and focused on my goals and tasks at hand.

953) My mindset has been improving every day and so has my life.

954) My purpose is filled with happiness, love, peace and bliss.

955) Success is my only option; failure will never be an option.

956) The day I get what I want, is the day that I will be happy.

957) The more responsibility I have, the better leader I become.

958) The more successful I become, the more knowledge I acquire.

959) The Universe is filled with unlimited possibilities for me.

960) This is my time to shine because my life is just beginning.

961) A good day for me is one where I feel better than yesterday.

962) All of my dreams and aspirations are coming true one by one.

963) All that matters in life can be found right here, right now.

964) Even when faced with challenges, I remain calm and positive.

965) Every day I think about how much money I will make tomorrow.

966) Every single day, I'm getting better and better at being me.

967) I am ready to work hard and committed to achieving my goals.

968) I carry myself like a manly man, and I get respect for this.

969) I enjoy my work, and feel successful in all my undertakings.

970) I have the power of attraction; everything good comes to me.

971) I take control of my own mind, and that is always my choice.

972) I trust my intuition to guide me towards love and happiness.

973) I welcome the most perfect of my creations into my life now.

974) If I love myself, then others will see that and love me too.

975) Life is not about yesterday; it's all about what I do today.

976) My blood is pumping through me, and it is pure testosterone.

977) My body is capable of anything so I will treat it with love.

978) My business and finance are doing incredibly well right now.

979) My mind is a powerful magnet that attracts to me all I need.

980) My mind is clear and calm, and I'm ready to take on the day.

981) The only limitations on my life are those I place on myself.

982) Today is a new day that holds infinite possibilities for me.

983) Today, I am going to learn how to speak with a deeper voice.

984) Today, I'm excited to take on all new challenges with gusto.

985) As long as I keep moving forward then everything is possible.

986) Every day I get a little better at whatever I put my mind to.

987) Every day is another chance to be the best version of myself.

988) Every day, people recognize my authority as a natural leader.

989) Every obstacle puts me one step closer to where I want to be.

990) I am a man who is bold and kind, knowing that people like me.

991) I am a man who loves and is loved, so I will always be happy.

992) I am a man's man, and I command power with every step I take.

993) I am good with women because I know who I am and what I want.

994) I am quick to respond with proportional force when necessary.

995) I am responsible for myself, my life, and the way it unfolds.

996) I deserve to be successful; everyone deserves something good.

997) I focus my attention on the solution rather than the problem.

998) I have faced many fears, and now I am ready to face new ones.

999) I have more than enough time to accomplish all that I desire.

1000) I know that there is greatness in me waiting to be unleashed.

11

Lesson XI. Presence

The warrior in you works hard every day of his life - because success doesn't come to those who wait; it comes to those who make the best use of their time. He knows that the only thing standing between him and his dreams is time, so he makes every moment count.

Challenge: Live in the present moment

To move forward toward a brighter future, we need to stop living in the past and worrying about mistakes that happened long ago. Everything in life is temporary, which means that everything around you is subject to change. This idea might be saddening at first, but if you embrace it, you'll be able to appreciate the moment for what it is.

It's important to live in the present moment because everything we do is a part of our journey throughout life. If we keep looking back and regretting the past, then we won't be able to learn from our mistakes and move forward. There's always something that we can improve on in our lives, so focus on how you're feeling right now instead of what happened to you long ago.

To start, try to focus on what you can see right now. This sounds simple, but when you're in a rush or thinking about something else, it can be easy to forget. Look around you and acknowledge the people and objects that are around you. You can even pretend that it's your first time at the place that you're currently in, which will allow you to learn more about it.

If you let the past control your present moment, then it'll have a significant impact on your future. So, try to embrace the idea of living in the present moment and see how much better everything becomes in your life.

If you have trouble doing this, you can pick up a meditation habit. Meditation is a great way to keep your mind focused on the present, which will allow you to find greater happiness and success in life.

Affirmations 1001-1100

1001) I will not fear failure because it is a natural part of life.

1002) I will not give up on my dreams, no matter how long it takes.

1003) I will not let things that I have no control over, affect me.

1004) I will not set limits for myself because I know my potential.

1005) My financial well-being is growing stronger every single day.

1006) My inner peace begins with forgiveness for myself and others.

1007) My inner wisdom allows me to see the best in every situation.

1008) My mind is always on the things that are working in my favor.

1009) My past does not define me; my future is bright with promise.

1010) My time will come even if it does not seem like it right now.

1011) No one can push me down because today is going to be awesome.

1012) The law of attraction brings all good into my life right now.

1013) The more opposition that comes my way, the stronger I become.

1014) The only way that I will fail is if I stop trying altogether.

1015) There is no better time than now to make my dreams come true.

1016) Today I must always do my best because my life depends on it.

1017) Today is the perfect day to begin making my life even better.

1018) When I work out, my testosterone levels increase dramatically.

1019) All of my relationships are loving, supportive and nourishing.

1020) Each day allows me to become better at what I do and who I am.

1021) Every day of my life has many wonderful gifts in store for me.

1022) I always think positive, and I am always happy no matter what.

1023) I am a hero of my own story, always fighting to save everyone.

1024) I am a man of purpose and honor, so I will strive to do good.

1025) I am a man who acts with strength, decisiveness and necessity.

1026) I am aware that there are some people who want to see me fail.

1027) I am destined for success because I am destined for greatness.

1028) I am responsible for my own happiness, success and well-being.

1029) I am the best man that ever lived because I refuse to give up.

1030) I am very conscious of the thoughts that I think all day long.

1031) I appreciate the power of my mind to direct me toward success.

1032) I cannot change the past but I can definitely shape my future.

1033) I easily command the attention and respect of those around me.

1034) I focus on what is most important and ignore the distractions.

1035) I forgive myself for not being perfect, it's okay to be human.

1036) I let go of feelings that are not mine and they will leave me.

1037) I love to learn about different people's cultures and beliefs.

1038) I will embrace change and use it as an opportunity for growth.

1039) If only others would love themselves as much as I love myself.

1040) I'm healthy in body and mind because my thoughts are positive.

1041) In order to succeed, I must first believe that it is possible.

1042) It's okay to dream big because big dreams lead to big results.

1043) Life is an adventure waiting to happen, and I am ready for it.

1044) Life loves to flow through me so life loves me no matter what.

1045) My income is increasing at an ideal rate for me and my family.

1046) My success will be measured by my happiness not anyone else's.

1047) My thoughts are filled with peace, love and harmony right now.

1048) No matter how long it takes, I will never lose hope in myself.

1049) No one can push me around because I am living life for myself.

1050) No one can push me around because they cannot control my mind.

1051) Success is my only option. I am successful at everything I do.

1052) The path that life takes me on is not up to anyone but myself.

1053) The world is mine; no one can stop me from taking what's mine.

1054) Every day of my life gets better and better starting right now.

1055) I am grateful for what I have and more will come to me as well.

1056) I am strong and capable of handling anything that comes my way.

1057) I am the master of my destiny so everything is possible for me.

1058) I am the only person that can stop me from achieving my dreams.

1059) I am unstoppable and no one can stop me from reaching my goals.

1060) I am willing to take responsibility for the quality of my life.

1061) I deserve the best in life, and it is my birthright to have it.

1062) I don't need to know everything right now; I can learn as I go.

1063) I have all the time in the world to do everything I want to do.

1064) I have the power to change anything about myself that I choose.

1065) I have the power to change my life by changing the way I think.

1066) I stand up for what's right, even when the odds are against me.

1067) I treat myself with love and respect and so does everyone else.

1068) I will always believe in my dreams and never give up on myself.

1069) I will not let my past determine what I can or cannot do today.

1070) I will use my mistakes as a lesson so they do not happen again.

1071) If an opportunity presents itself, I will give it my best shot.

1072) If you want to succeed in life, never let failure be an option.

1073) In this very moment something wonderful will happen in my life.

1074) Life gets better every day so today might be the best day ever.

1075) My body is strong, my mind is sharp, and my spirit is powerful.

1076) My future is so much brighter because I am surrounded by light.

1077) My life is full of abundance, love, joy, happiness, and health.

1078) My mind is focused on positive, uplifting thoughts and actions.

1079) My potential is limitless because I refuse to believe it isn't.

1080) My shoulders and arms are getting bigger and stronger every day.

1081) No one can tell me what to do - I am the master of my own life.

1082) People love my energy; they find it contagious and interesting.

1083) The higher my testosterone levels are, the more alpha I become.

1084) The only person who is standing in the way of my success is me.

1085) The pain from yesterday is gone, it is now time to enjoy today.

1086) The sky is the limit for human beings, no matter what they say.

1087) The time is now to be the best version of myself that I can be.

1088) The world needs what I have to offer and I am happy to give it.

1089) Today I will consciously receive success, health and happiness.

1090) What was yesterday is behind me today, never to haunt me again.

1091) When life gets me down, I look for the good in every situation.

1092) I deserve to be successful and abundant in all areas of my life.

1093) Every day that passes by is one step closer to where I want to be.

1094) Everything is going to be okay because I am confident in myself.

1095) I allow everything that happens to me to be for my highest good.

1096) I am a wonderful and amazing person; I deserve the best in life.

1097) I am always in the mood to have fun and do whatever I feel like.

1098) I am one of life's success stories. And the best is yet to come.

1099) I am one with life and life is flowing through every part of me.

1100) I approach problems from a place of calmness and insightfulness.

12

Lesson XII. Conflict

The warrior in you doesn't let anyone push him around - because he's the only one who gets to decide how he is going to let people treat him. He stands up for himself and respects others regardless of their position in the social hierarchy.

Challenge: Set boundaries

Set boundaries with people in your life who drain your energy or make you feel bad about yourself.

You need to realize that people have different personalities and that they think differently from you. There are some who'll be happy when you achieve your goals, but there will always be those who seek to tear down the progress of others.

If someone in your life always makes you feel bad about yourself or try to control you, it's time for a change. It might be time to end the relationship, but if you're unsure of what to do, it's best to communicate with them about your feelings.

Tell them how they make you feel and express why their behavior is harmful to your well-being. If they care about you, they'll most likely respect your boundaries and stop with their negative behavior.

If they don't stop, then it means that they are not worth your time or effort. You should move on from them with no regrets or at least drastically reduce your interactions with them. Do this for your own sake, because you deserve the best in life.

Affirmations 1101-1200

1101) I deserve happiness, and I will fight for it until the very end.

1102) I deserve the best and today I take steps toward manifesting it.

1103) I find the opportunities to help others no matter how busy I am.

1104) I have it in my power to achieve anything that I put my mind to.

1105) I have the power to be, have and do anything that I can imagine.

1106) I make the best decisions because I genuinely care about myself.

1107) I take full responsibility for my choices and experiences today.

1108) I will act now on all ideas that can move me closer to my goals.

1109) I will continue to make progress no matter how slow it may seem.

1110) I work hard every day to be the best version of myself possible.

1111) It's okay to feel upset, because that is how I release the pain.

1112) Life has a way of taking care of things when we least expect it.

1113) My inner-strength gives me the power to be happy no matter what.

1114) My life is filled with happiness, love, peace and joy right now.

1115) My mind is my best friend; it helps me achieve all of my dreams.

1116) My mistakes are opportunities for me to learn and become better.

1117) My purpose is to be the best version of myself every single day.

1118) My thoughts, words and actions always benefit myself and others.

1119) My words carry great power - they support me and inspire others.

1120) No matter what they say about me I know the truth, I am awesome.

1121) Success is nothing more than hard work that pays off in the end.

1122) The world belongs to me because I know who I am and what I want.

1123) Today, I am grateful for all of the wonderful people in my life.

1124) When I feel unstoppable today, there is nothing to slow me down.

1125) Why wait until tomorrow when happiness can actually begin today?

1126) Love fills my heart now. All because of how I feel about myself.

1127) As I take care of myself, life gets better for everyone else too.

1128) Doing the best that I can in every moment is what makes me proud.

1129) Every day in every way, my mind is getting stronger and stronger.

1130) Every time I stand up straight and tall, I become more confident.

1131) Everything I want to achieve in life is now well within my reach.

1132) Everything that happens to me provides me with a valuable lesson.

1133) I am a gift to this world, so I will spread love everywhere I go.

1134) I am a success in my own eyes; no one can take this away from me.

1135) I am a winner and I can achieve anything that I truly believe in.

1136) I am grateful for the opportunities that life has given me today.

1137) I am here for a reason, no matter how hard it may seem right now.

1138) I am unstoppable and nothing can stop me from achieving my goals.

1139) I attract loving people into my life who enhance it in every way.

1140) I give as much as I can, whenever I can to those that deserve it.

1141) I give myself permission to have an amazing day every single day.

1142) I have everything it takes to be successful at what I love to do.

1143) I love myself. All others are mirrors of my attitude toward life.

1144) I release testosterone through my sweat glands while working out.

1145) I take care of myself and do things that make me happy every day.

1146) I will never stop learning because that's what life is all about.

1147) I will not let the actions of others affect me in a negative way.

1148) I will trust my gut because it has never steered me wrong before.

1149) In every area of my life, I am becoming more and more successful.

1150) My body does not define who I am; my heart and soul are my temple.

1151) My destiny is within grasp now that I have clarity on what it is.

1152) My heart is big enough to hold the love of everyone in the world.

1153) My life is filled with happiness, love, peace and joy, right now.

1154) My money situation has become tremendously improved in every way.

1155) My muscles are more defined than ever before, and it feels great.

1156) My personality is magnetic everyone always wants to be around me.

1157) My success does not come at the expense of anyone else's failure.

1158) No matter how lonely life may seem; I will never give up on love.

1159) Successful people don't wait for opportunities; they create them.

1160) The more I love myself, the more everyone around me loves me too.

1161) The more that I help people, the more successful my life becomes.

1162) The power to succeed lies in me so today success can be achieved.

1163) The power within me cannot be extinguished by anyone or anything.

1164) The world is in my hands because I know who I am and what I want.

1165) There is room for only one thought in my mind: "The perfect way."

1166) Today I will do the things that others have been asking me to do.

1167) When I give my best to everything, I always get the best results.

1168) When I set my mind on achieving something - anything is possible.

1169) I am one with the world - I am one with abundance and prosperity.

1170) My life gets easier with time because I get wiser with experience.

1171) A positive mind will lead me to lasting happiness and inner peace.

1172) Every day that goes by, my future gets just a little bit brighter.

1173) Every day, I get stronger and more powerful than the previous day.

1174) Every day brings new opportunities for self-improvement and growth.

1175) Everything in life has a meaning even if I can't see it right now.

1176) I am a man of the world; my voice is worldly, commanding and sexy.

1177) I am always in control of my life no matter what people may think.

1178) I am committed to helping others become healthy and happy as well.

1179) I am committed to making my life as awesome as it can possibly be.

1180) I make positive choices each day that bring me closer to my goals.

1181) I will always protect the people I love because they are my world.

1182) It's okay to make mistakes, because that is how we learn and grow.

1183) Life is like a book and every day I'm writing something new in it.

1184) My confidence is solid like a rock, unshakable like Mount Everest.

1185) My daily habits help me be more confident and happier with myself.

1186) My family always has my back and they are supportive of my dreams.

1187) My masculinity comes from within, not from the approval of others.

1188) No matter what problems I face, I always find a way to solve them.

1189) Nothing can stop me from achieving my goals today; nothing at all.

1190) The more successful I become; the less time I have for negativity.

1191) The only thing better than today is the tomorrow that it leads to.

1192) The positive energy flowing through my body heals all parts of me.

1193) The world is better with me in it because I'm the best part of it.

1194) Today is a new day and it holds countless blessings for my future.

1195) Today will be a great day because I am choosing it to be that way.

1196) When I see a woman that looks great, I will make her a compliment.

1197) When I stay positive, I will attract positive things into my life.

1198) Divine guidance flows through me now, helping me make good choices.

1199) Each day my body changes more and more into a masculine powerhouse.

1200) Every day is a new adventure, whether I am the hero or the villain.

13

Lesson XIII. Honor

The warrior in you has a code of honor - that includes loyalty, integrity and strength. He knows that honor doesn't mean being perfect, but rather doing what's right even when nobody is watching.

Challenge: Break out of the prison of expectations

Stop making excuses for your self-limiting beliefs and free yourself from the prison of kowtowing to other people's rules, expectations, and fears. When we let other people tell us how to live and what to believe, we create a prison of apathy for ourselves. We become trapped by other people's beliefs about reality, which can keep us from our dreams.

When you start to break free of the prison of expectations, it's important to focus on your own goals. It's not about defying what other people want for you, but focusing on what you need in life.

If someone has a problem with the life that you're trying to build for yourself, then let them deal with it. You don't have to try and change their mind or even justify your actions to them. As long as you're living up to your standards, then that's all the matters in life.

You can't control what other people think or do, but you can change your perspective on how things should be. Don't let other people's thoughts or actions change your goals, but instead use those experiences as lessons for why you're doing what you're doing.

When you take the time to reflect on the way that you live your life, you'll find that this perspective will allow you to live a happier and more fulfilling lifestyle. You deserve to have people in your life who appreciate you for who you are, so stop seeking appreciation of those who don't see how amazing of a person you truly are.

Affirmations 1201-1300

1201) Every day, in every way, everywhere, I'm getting better and better.

1202) I always find time to exercise, even when it's just for 10 minutes.

1203) I always see the best in others and they always see the best in me.

1204) I am a magnet for good health, good fortune and good relationships.

1205) I am a powerful creator of my own destiny from this moment forward.

1206) I am a powerful sexual being because of the testosterone within me.

1207) I am a unique person with great gifts that the world needs from me.

1208) I am open to receiving great opportunities that are heading my way.

1209) I am perfect for the situation I occupy now, and I grow constantly.

1210) I am powerful beyond measure because I am capable of self- control.

1211) I am strong, and capable and confident in my actions and decisions.

1212) I forgive others for what they have done to the best of my ability.

1213) I walk with masculine swag because my testosterone levels are high.

1214) I will make someone's day today because it is in my power to do so.

1215) I will never stop fighting for my dreams because they are worth it.

1216) I will not allow someone else's judgement influence who I am today.

1217) I will not let a bad day make me forget what a good day feels like.

1218) I will not let my emotions prevent me from achieving success today.

1219) I will use the life I was given to make a difference in this world.

1220) It's okay if I don't know everything yet because nobody is perfect.

1221) Just because I made a mistake, it doesn't mean that I am a failure.

1222) Life is tough sometimes; it's not meant for me to go through alone.

1223) My attitude determines what kind of day I will experience tomorrow.

1224) My brain is my most valuable asset and I will treat it accordingly.

1225) My happiness grows more and more each day, hour, minute and second.

1226) My life is full of challenge because that's what makes me stronger.

1227) My past does not define me because my future is what determines me.

1228) My past does not define me. Today is a new day and a new beginning.

1229) No job is ever too big for me to handle because I love a challenge.

1230) No matter what happens, I will stay strong and keep moving forward.

1231) Only those who can see the invisible, can do the impossible for me.

1232) The world around me becomes more manly because I am more masculine.

1233) The world does not owe me anything, but I owe the world everything.

1234) There is a reason for everything that happens in my life right now.

1235) You can't make everyone happy because everyone has different needs.

1236) My thoughts are creative and they bring me abundance beyond measure.

1237) All of my dreams are coming true because I see the signs everywhere.

1238) By the end of today, my life is going to be better than ever before.

1239) Celebrating success propels me into new heights of self-fulfillment.

1240) Divine energy flows through me now, filling my spirit with pure joy.

1241) Each day that goes by I become stronger, more confident and focused.

1242) Every day I am learning something new about my body and how it works.

1243) Good things happen to me every day and tomorrow will be even better.

1244) I am a positive person who spreads positivity to everyone around me.

1245) I am able to relax knowing that everything will work out in the end.

1246) I am surrounded by loving supportive people from this moment onward.

1247) I deserve the best, and today is a day for me to let my light shine.

1248) I deserve to be in a position of power and control over my own life.

1249) I have come a long way, and it's all thanks to my humble beginnings.

1250) I have worked hard for everything that I have, and I am proud of it.

1251) I respect myself and other people show me strong amounts of respect.

1252) I will do what needs to be done today, because I am a man of honor.

1253) My anger is not a weakness, but rather an expression of my strength.

1254) My mind is always full of positive thoughts that bring me happiness.

1255) My mind is always on the job. It never wanders, daydreams or doubts.

1256) My past does not dictate my future because I choose happiness today.

1257) My positive thoughts trigger my mind to work for me, not against me.

1258) My thoughts are powerful and they manifest themselves in my reality.

1259) Obstacles are meant to be overcome; they are not meant to defeat me.

1260) The more that I give of myself, the more that life gives back to me.

1261) The past has passed; the future is here. And all that exists is NOW.

1262) There is nothing that can stop me from being great, not even myself.

1263) Today I will focus my energy on creating positive change in my life.

1264) Today is all about me because nobody is going to save me but myself.

1265) When I focus on being productive, everything in my life gets better.

1266) Most people don't like change but change is inevitable so embrace it.

1267) Everything that happened to me today is exactly the way it should be.

1268) All I need to do today is relax and let life happen as it pleases me.

1269) I am always taken care of in the right way at exactly the right time.

1270) I am becoming the best man that I can possibly be, and it feels good.

1271) I am comfortable with who I am today, no matter how I may be feeling.

1272) I am loved by many people, especially the important women in my life.

1273) I am strong enough to overcome any challenge that comes my way today.

1274) I create my own destiny and nothing stops me from achieving my goals.

1275) I have everything it takes to be successful in the things I do today.

1276) I have made the right choices today, because I know myself very well.

1277) I know that it is okay to be dominant in my relationships with women.

1278) I make difficult things look easy, because everything is easy for me.

1279) If I believe in myself, nothing can stop me from achieving greatness.

1280) Infinite power flows through me now, creating peace within me always.

1281) Life is filled with many ups and downs but I will always get back up.

1282) My greatest, most wonderful successes are now manifesting in my life.

1283) My mind is focused on the present moment and my goals for the future.

1284) My present state of mind is one of useful enthusiasm and high energy.

1285) My skills are improving every day because I am determined to succeed.

1286) My success will not depend on the economy, but rather my own efforts.

1287) My work creates value for others and makes a difference in the world.

1288) No matter how difficult things seem, there is always a positive side.

1289) Nothing in life is more important than the actions that I take today.

1290) People who say it cannot be done should not interrupt those doing it.

1291) Success in life is when you do what you love and get paid for it too.

1292) The future is bright because my actions today are adding light to it.

1293) The strength of my decisions becomes greater each moment that passes.

1294) The universe provides everything I need in order to pursue happiness.

1295) Today, I have achieved everything I ever wanted and it feels so good.

1296) Today, I will not envy anyone else's success because today is my day.

1297) When I believe in myself and my abilities, I can accomplish anything.

1298) When life gives me lemons, I make lemonade and succeed in every area.

1299) All of the lessons that I learn in life will benefit me at some point.

1300) All the people that I love are also there for me whenever I need them.

14

Lesson XIV. Consistency

The warrior in you always follows through - because he takes responsibility for his actions and doesn't make excuses for them. He never makes promises he can't keep or accept assignments that will put him in a bad position. In the heat of battle, he does what needs to be done regardless of the consequences.

Challenge: Be a strong mind in a strong body

Be fit and healthy so that you can awaken your inner badass. The stronger your mind and body are, the more likely it is for you to accomplish your goals in life. Working on yourself physically has a huge impact on your mental health, because when you're in better shape, you tend to feel happier.

There are many ways that you can improve your physical health. You can start with little things like getting more sleep and eating better, because doing so will give you more energy to take on each day.

Working out can be a great way to release stress and improve your mental health, because the endorphins released by your brain during exercise help it to function better. If you can, try finding a workout buddy who'll hold you accountable for working out on a regular basis because having that accountability will motivate you more to stay committed.

Choosing to take care of yourself both physically and mentally will have a positive impact on your life in many ways. Not only will your life be more fulfilling, but you'll also have a better chance of living it to the fullest.

Try to improve all aspects of your life during this month by working on yourself physically. If you decide to start a new fitness program, you should decide to stick to it for 30 days. If you decide to eat healthier, then try to implement that for the entire month. If you focus on a goal for 30 days straight with a positive mindset and determination, then you'll find that your overall quality of life will drastically improve.

Affirmations 1301-1400

1301) Each day that passes brings me closer to the person that I want to be.

1302) Every day is a gift and today I choose to live the best possible life.

1303) Every day, I make choices that support me in becoming more successful.

1304) Every new day brings with it a new sense of purpose for me to live by.

1305) I always have the power to choose how I feel and think about anything.

1306) I am a successful person because I have learned from my past mistakes.

1307) I am calm and relaxed; I have plenty of time to get things done today.

1308) I am fearless and unstoppable because I know who I am and what I want.

1309) I am handsome and wonderful and people like me more than they realize.

1310) I am not afraid to be ambitious and confident when pursuing my dreams.

1311) I am on a mission of greatness; everything I touch turns into success.

1312) I become more successful with every step that I take towards my goals.

1313) I can do anything within my power, and trust the rest to the universe.

1314) I cultivate my sexual energy, but I never take it too far with others.

1315) I deserve all good things life has to offer, including perfect health.

1316) I have all the tools I need to be successful, so today will be my day.

1317) I learn something new every day because life is full of possibilities.

1318) I trust in the universe to deliver what I need exactly when I need it.

1319) I will do what it takes to get where I want to be, no one can stop me.

1320) I will never give up on my dreams so long as I keep believing in them.

1321) I will not let fear get the better of me because I have all the power.

1322) I will not let the fear of failure or change stop me from being great.

1323) If no one believes in me, then it is okay because I believe in myself.

1324) It doesn't matter what happens, I will remain positive and optimistic.

1325) It is easy for me to achieve and maintain a fit and healthy lifestyle.

1326) It is my choice whether or not I let the opinions of others affect me.

1327) It's not about what I want to achieve but rather who I want to become.

1328) Life is an adventure and today is a new chapter waiting to be written.

1329) Life is easier when you focus on the solution rather than the problem.

1330) Life is full of surprises, but I'm always prepared for the unexpected.

1331) My inner strength allows me to persevere in the face of any challenge.

1332) My mind is calm; my body is relaxed; my soul is one with the universe.

1333) No matter how many mistakes I make, I am still worthy of great things.

1334) No one can intimidate me because I have no fear of anything or anyone.

1335) No one can push me down because every day I get stronger and stronger.

1336) Positive thoughts create a positive future; this is a universal truth.

1337) The longer I breathe this fresh air, the taller and stronger I become.

1338) Time is a commodity that cannot be bought with money so use it wisely.

1339) Today will be another great day because every day is a blessing to me.

1340) Today, I am living the life of a happy, healthy, wealthy and wise man.

1341) All I need to do is focus on what's important, and keep moving forward.

1342) As a man, I must always stand tall and be strong for those whom I love.

1343) Every day is a brand-new beginning, so I will start with a fresh slate.

1344) Every single day is a chance to reinvent myself so I will do just that.

1345) I accept my past, learn from it, and move forward into a better future.

1346) I am better than everyone else because I am the best version of myself.

1347) I am doing the best that I can with who I am, and where I am right now.

1348) I am most happy when I find new opportunities to grow as an individual.

1349) I am not afraid of anything in this world because I control my destiny.

1350) I am now experiencing all the joy and happiness that life has to offer.

1351) I am worthy of good things coming my way because I always ask for them.

1352) I choose to focus on the good things in life instead of the bad things.

1353) I push myself to succeed because I know that I am capable of greatness.

1354) I radiate peace, joy and love to all with whom I come in contact today.

1355) I take action, even when I do not want to, and accomplish great things.

1356) I will love myself for who I am and treat others with the same respect.

1357) I will succeed; nothing and no one can stop me from achieving my goals.

1358) If I see it, then I believe it; and if I believe it, then I achieve it.

1359) If you want something, don't just wish for it, go out there and get it.

1360) It's time for me to get up and go so I can live the life I dream about.

1361) Loving myself is the foundation for all other relationships in my life.

1362) My faith in my abilities makes me unstoppable, nothing can stop me now.

1363) My income is constantly increasing as I move towards financial success.

1364) My mind is capable of manifesting anything; it has unlimited potential.

1365) My thoughts always contribute to the highest good of myself and others.

1366) My work is filled with joy and ease as I remain calm and serene within.

1367) Someone is watching me today, so I will show them what good looks like.

1368) Sometimes life gets tough, but that's okay because it makes me tougher.

1369) The best way to improve my life is to make other people's lives better.

1370) The more that I help other people, the more successful my life becomes.

1371) The only way to achieve my goals is through hard work and perseverance.

1372) The world is my oyster. I'm going to be the best man I can possibly be.

1373) There is no reason for me to argue because I am not at war with anyone.

1374) Today is better than yesterday, and tomorrow will be better than today.

1375) When I feel overwhelmed, I will take deep breaths and calm myself down.

1376) When I focus on my goals, nothing gets in my way. Success comes easily.

1377) When you really believe in yourself, there's nothing that can stop you.

1378) Being positive is an attractive quality, so I must always stay that way.

1379) I am becoming more and more of a man with each and every passing second.

1380) I am determined to achieve my goals no matter how much time it takes me.

1381) I am never alone because my angels and spirit guides are always with me.

1382) I am ready to release all that does not serve my higher purpose in life.

1383) I am thankful for all my past because it has led me to where I am today.

1384) I command my mind to focus so intensely on what is most important to me.

1385) I use laughter as a way to release my full emotions and enjoy life more.

1386) I will always do my best because this attitude makes life easier for me.

1387) I will learn from my mistakes and move forward without fear in my heart.

1388) If I want to achieve success, I must begin believing that it's possible.

1389) If you think in a positive way, then only positive things happen to you.

1390) In every way possible, I am becoming a better man today than yesteryear.

1391) It is not my duty to make others happy but rather to be a reason for it.

1392) My family is proud of me and they are there for me whenever I need them.

1393) My manliness and honor encompass and protect my family and those I love.

1394) My mind is strong and powerful - free from doubt, worry, guilt and fear.

1395) My past has made me who I am today and I love myself more because of it.

1396) My past is only a foundation for where I am today; I do not dwell on it.

1397) My thoughts create my reality so today; I will only think good thoughts.

1398) My work is absolutely perfect for me, just the way that it is right now.

1399) Obstacles will come but they do not define who I am, only my actions do.

1400) Only I have control over my life and I can do incredible things with it.

15

Lesson XV. Risk

The warrior in you takes calculated risks - because he knows that no matter how bad things are, they could always be worse. He also doesn't give up simply because something is difficult. The bigger the challenge, the greater his determination to overcome it.

Challenge: Take a calculated risk

You won't be able to grow as a person if you always play it safe, because playing it safe only allows the fear of failure to control your life. In order to accomplish something worthwhile in life, you're going to have to take risks and push out of your comfort zone.

This doesn't mean that you need to go skydiving or bungee jumping; it simply means that you take calculated risks in your life. Sometimes, the scariest thing about taking risks is thinking about what could happen if things don't work out how you planned.

Every time that you do something new, there's always the risk of failing and making a fool of yourself. If you are very risk-averse, then you probably feel very uncomfortable in these kinds of situations. The most important thing to do with this type of fear is recognize it so that you can push past it.

If something comes up in your life where you're required to take a risk, but you don't want to because of the potential consequences, then just think about why you feel so uncomfortable. Once you can pinpoint the root of this fear, it'll be easier to take a step in the right direction.

Taking calculated risks will help you to learn more about yourself and grow as a person while also helping you accomplish your goals in life. By taking small chances on an everyday basis, like trying something new or meeting new people, you'll become a much more interesting and well-rounded person.

If you don't know where to start, talk to five strangers over the next week and learn something interesting about each of them. By taking small chances like this, you'll start to feel less anxious about doing new things.

Affirmations 1401-1500

1401) People admire me and want to be like me, and it fills me with happiness.

1402) Successful people make money. It's not the money making them successful.

1403) The more that I live in alignment with my purpose, the better life gets.

1404) The next few years will bring me new challenges to meet with enthusiasm.

1405) Today I am going to stay positive even if my circumstances are negative.

1406) Today I choose to love who I am unconditionally, no matter what happens.

1407) Today, it's all about loving myself, then sharing that love with others.

1408) Be relentless with your life because life is too short for anything else.

1409) Each day is another chance at success as long as I put in my best effort.

1410) Every day I choose to have an awesome mindset; words cannot bring me down.

1411) Every moment in life has a way of teaching me something new about myself.

1412) I am a man of my word so I will do whatever it takes to keep my promises.

1413) I am a winner and that cannot change no matter what my circumstances are.

1414) I am becoming an increasingly more loving, compassionate and patient man.

1415) I am good enough the way that I am, and no one can tell me any different.

1416) I am here to live life on my own terms, and no one can tell me otherwise.

1417) I am more prepared than anyone else to achieve my dreams and aspirations.

1418) I deserve to be happy, healthy, and successful in all aspects of my life.

1419) I deserve to be rich and I create wealth with my thoughts and my actions.

1420) I have a strong will to succeed at whatever challenges are put before me.

1421) I have a vast network of people who support and care about my well-being.

1422) I have the power to change any area of my life that isn't working for me.

1423) I see myself with healthy eyes, knowing the strength of my mind and body.

1424) I will not give in to society's social pressures of what a man should be.

1425) I will not judge myself for my past mistakes, but rather learn from them.

1426) If I have money, I will spend it on things that are important to my life.

1427) Life is about enjoying my journey rather than rushing to the finish line.

1428) My ability is limited only by the amount of work that I am willing to do.

1429) No matter how great my problems may seem; I always find a way to succeed.

1430) No matter what happens, I know that there is a solution to every problem.

1431) No matter where I am, I will become the most powerful person in the room.

1432) No one can tell me what to do or say because they cannot control my mind.

1433) Success is always possible if you believe in yourself and your abilities.

1434) The more I help and support others; the better things come back to me.

1435) There is nothing in life that I cannot accomplish if I believe in myself.

1436) Today I am open to receiving great opportunities that are heading my way.

1437) Today I awaken into new possibilities as I see myself achieving my goals.

1438) Today, I let go of my past and step into the greatness that is my future.

1439) Today, money comes to me at the speed of light and in increasing amounts.

1440) When I see other people achieve success, it motivates me towards success.

1441) When times are tough, all I have to do is look within myself for answers.

1442) I am disciplined. Disciplined living brings success to all areas of life.

1443) All I see is opportunity, all I feel is excitement, all I know is success.

1444) Every day I become better at my craft as I learn from the world around me.

1445) Every hour of every day holds great promise for an exciting new beginning.

1446) I am a man of simple desires and I only require enough money to meet them.

1447) I am confident, I am powerful, and I can achieve anything that I focus on.

1448) I am doing my best with what I have so that someday soon, it will be more.

1449) I am doing the best that I can in every moment, no one could ask for more.

1450) I am not afraid to do what it takes to build a successful life for myself.

1451) I am successful because I put in the hard work necessary to be successful.

1452) I am the only one in control of my life so I will make this day a success.

1453) I am the only one who can stop myself from achieving success, nobody else.

1454) I deserve to be richly blessed abundantly with all good things in my life.

1455) I have been through a lot in life but that just means that I am resilient.

1456) I have the courage to be happy, so I will never shy away from feeling joy.

1457) I have the power to take control over everything that shows up in my life.

1458) I must allow myself to live for me because the world is full of judgement.

1459) I now attract positive people into my life, and that's just the beginning.

1460) I will not punish myself because someone else thinks I am not good enough.

1461) I yearn for more; this ambition fuels me to keep getting better every day.

1462) If you take risks, then at least make sure that they are calculated risks.

1463) It does not matter what people think about me as long as I do not give up.

1464) It doesn't matter what others think of me, because I know who I really am.

1465) My muscles ripple and bulge, and other people notice my newfound strength.

1466) My strength guides me forward on my path to manifesting all that I desire.

1467) My true self is intelligent, powerful, loving, kind, generous and patient.

1468) No matter how bad things may seem, there is always a lesson to be learned.

1469) No matter what happens, I know that everything will work out for the best.

1470) People are always giving to me in wonderful and unexpected ways right now.

1471) The more that I do for myself, the more that success will come back to me.

1472) The more that I let go of negative people in my life, the better off I am.

1473) The seed of greatness lives inside of me, no one can stop it from growing.

1474) The world is open to me and I have the potential to do great things in it.

1475) Today is another day where I can be the change I want to see in the world.

1476) Today, I have achieved everything I have ever wanted and it feels so good.

1477) Today, tomorrow, and every day after that I grow more confident in myself.

1478) A positive mind means everything, don't ever let anyone tell you otherwise.

1479) Even though I may not see it today, what is meant for me will be mine soon.

1480) Every day in every way, I grow stronger and more powerful than ever before.

1481) Every day, my life becomes more and more complete as new blessings show up.

1482) I am confident in my abilities and will never stop until I get what I want.

1483) I am filled with excitement and energy that cannot be contained, right now.

1484) I am unstoppable because I'm on a mission to be the best version of myself.

1485) I don't have time for people who are not supportive of my dreams and goals.

1486) I feel detached from all past events that do not serve my highest good now.

1487) I feel happy and content right now because I always do what's right for me.

1488) I have mastered self-discipline so that my future can remain in my control.

1489) I will continue to grow stronger day after day even if there is resistance.

1490) I will give myself a chance to prove that I am good enough for what I want.

1491) I will set myself free from toxic people who drain my energy and happiness.

1492) It's not about what happens to me, but how I react to it that matters most.

1493) My income increases every day as I become more valuable to those around me.

1494) My inner resolve is stronger than any obstacle that life can put in my way.

1495) My joy is of such high quality that it spills over onto everyone around me.

1496) My subconscious mind is strong and powerful, directing me towards my goals.

1497) The more challenges that I face head on, the less fear shows up in my life.

1498) The more difficulty I have in growing up, the more magical my life becomes.

1499) The more that I make use of my talents, the more opportunities come my way.

1500) With each passing day, I become stronger and wiser and better at what I do.

16

Lesson XVI. Authenticity

The warrior in you never tries to be someone else - because he knows that people will only see the real him. He doesn't try to imitate others or simply copy their success because he wants to be his own man and his own self.

Challenge: Accept yourself as a man

Accept yourself for who you are and learn to love all the qualities that make you unique. The more you accept yourself for who you are, the more others will be able to love and appreciate you as well.

The way that you think of yourself is one of the most important aspects of your life. If you are constantly putting yourself down, then this will have a negative impact on your self-esteem and confidence.

One of the biggest parts of improving your attitude about yourself is to learn to laugh at things that used to bother you. Don't take every situation so seriously and be willing to admit when you're wrong.

Be confident in yourself and your abilities, even if other people don't agree. If you go through life with a positive mindset about who you are, then it'll make everything else in your life easier. The more that you challenge yourself to become a better person, the more opportunities will come your way.

Do not let society or other people drag you down for who you are supposed to be. You are a man, and that is something that you should be proud of. Try being yourself while also challenging yourself to become a better person. By taking control of who you are as a man, you'll find that your life will become so much better.

Affirmations 1501-1600

1501) I create my own reality with every single thought that springs from my mind.

1502) A positive mental attitude gives me the power to be the person I want to be.

1503) I cannot let my past dictate my future because that is where growth happens.

1504) I don't mind trying again, as long as I know for sure that I gave it my all.

1505) I embrace the challenge, and my fear diminishes with every step that I take.

1506) I feel like a man, and my masculine energy radiates through everyone I meet.

1507) I have the ability to follow through on my ideas and see them to completion.

1508) I trust my instincts to guide me because I am the man in control of my life.

1509) I will protect my heart because it's the one thing that keeps my body alive.

1510) Just because something is hard to accomplish doesn't mean it isn't possible.

1511) Life is an endless opportunity for me to learn and evolve into a better man.

1512) My future is filled with countless opportunities for success and prosperity.

1513) People are not perfect, but that does not mean I should be critical of them.

1514) The more I love myself the more loving relationships will come into my life.

1515) When life knocks me down, I will get back up again and continue being great.

1516) Each day brings me an opportunity to become a better man than the day before.

1517) Every day I'm hustling a little harder because that's what life is all about.

1518) I am doing everything in my power to make my future the best time of my life.

1519) I am more than just a conqueror; I am an inspiration to others who dream big.

1520) I am powerful beyond measure and no one can stop me from achieving greatness.

1521) I deserve all the good that life has to offer and it's up to me to go get it.

1522) I forgive myself for all past mistakes, and I do not judge myself in any way.

1523) I will not let my fears stop me from becoming who life intended for me to be.

1524) I'm getting better and better at letting go of anger, hatred, and negativity.

1525) It is normal to have fear, but my fear is not nearly as strong as my courage.

1526) It is okay to make mistakes because sometimes they are the best way to learn.

1527) My life is full of dreams so today I will make those dreams become a reality.

1528) My love for people gives me an understanding that others lack to some degree.

1529) My mind is more powerful than anything else; it's up to me what I do with it.

1530) People are naturally drawn to me; they trust my intuition and follow my lead.

1531) People love seeing me happy and when I am, it rubs off on everyone around me.

1532) The first hour of the day is the rudder on a ship; each new day is the ocean.

1533) When I truly want something, the entire universe conspires to make it happen.

1534) An amazing life lies ahead of me as long as I am willing to put in the effort.

1535) Before I can achieve success, I must first believe that it is possible for me.

1536) Each day brings new opportunities for me to grow and evolve into a better man.

1537) Each day, I become stronger and smarter as I face any obstacle in front of me.

1538) I am a man of integrity and honesty, knowing that it makes all the difference.

1539) I am a man of patience and take my time with things until they are done right.

1540) I am confident in my ability to achieve anything that I set out to accomplish.

1541) I am focused on achieving my goals; committed to the path that leads me there.

1542) I am intensely focused on achieving my goals, no matter how many times I fail.

1543) I can say no whenever someone asks me to do something that doesn't feel right.

1544) I cannot control everything but I can definitely be in control of my thoughts.

1545) I earn enough money at what I do to meet all of my needs and some of my wants.

1546) I have a positive outlook on this day and everything that happens to me today.

1547) I have done a lot of things right in my life, even if it doesn't seem like it.

1548) I have no need to try and be someone else because my being is already awesome.

1549) I have so much to be grateful for right now, and I will never stop showing it.

1550) I must not think of myself as a failure because life is full of ups and downs.

1551) I think about what I want but I also consider what will happen if I do get it.

1552) I will never give up, there is no such thing as a failure until I quit trying.

1553) I will not let my past dictate who I am or how I live out the rest of my life.

1554) It doesn't matter what I go through in life because it only makes me stronger.

1555) My best is my ability to adapt and overcome any challenge that life brings me.

1556) My confidence turns women on because of my inner strength and my testosterone.

1557) My discipline is unbreakable, my work ethic indomitable, my focus razor-sharp.

1558) My happiness depends on my thinking. I think only the best, and it will be so.

1559) Resistance is a sign that I am doing something right, so keep pushing forward.

1560) Success only comes to those who work hard and I will never shy away from that.

1561) The best time ever started right now and it is not going to stop anytime soon.

1562) The more I get out of my comfort zone, the more I am able to expand my limits.

1563) To have a positive mind means everything so today I will have a positive mind.

1564) Today I will focus on self-improvement and nothing will distract me from that.

1565) What I do today is important, because I am exchanging a day of my life for it.

1566) When life knocks me down, I pick myself up and act like nothing ever happened.

1567) When someone tries to bring me down, it only makes me want to fly even higher.

1568) All those who do evil will be brought down to their knees by the power of good.

1569) Every second of each day is an opportunity for me to grow and improve as a man.

1570) Every single day, I am growing as a person and becoming the best that I can be.

1571) Excuses are for losers but winners never make excuses, they make things happen.

1572) Greater than any fear and obstacle, is my courage and determination to succeed.

1573) I am a man with a purpose in life and every action of mine serves this purpose.

1574) I am becoming healthier and healthier each day managed by my healthy lifestyle.

1575) I am filled with potential that is overflowing, all I have to do is embrace it.

1576) I am much better today than I was last year, and next year will be even better.

1577) I am unstoppable right now; nothing can stop me from achieving greatness today.

1578) I focus on making fewer mistakes so that I can continue living an amazing life.

1579) I know that everything I am going through right now is only making me stronger.

1580) I love the person that I am today and will work to become even better tomorrow.

1581) I rise above the challenges and defeats of my life, with an unbreakable spirit.

1582) I will always give my best because that is what has gotten me this far in life.

1583) I will not be afraid to take the next step towards my goals because I am brave.

1584) I will not let go of my dreams because someone else thinks they are impossible.

1585) My body is changing into the type of masculine powerhouse that women just love.

1586) My enemies will never succeed in stopping me from progressing towards my goals.

1587) My life is a work in progress, and today is a great day to make it even better.

1588) My life is like a blowing wind, effortlessly going in the direction of success.

1589) My life is not my destination; it's my journey. And I enjoy every minute of it.

1590) My mind is always open to new possibilities that bring happiness into my world.

1591) My thoughts are focused on building a better life for myself and my loved ones.

1592) My time is very valuable, but I give myself permission to relax and enjoy life.

1593) No matter how bad of a day today might be, I know that tomorrow will be better.

1594) No matter what happens in life, it is already recorded; I either win or I learn.

1595) The more successful people I surround myself with the more successful I become.

1596) Today I choose to look at what I have instead of focusing on what I don't have.

1597) Today is going to be an amazing day because I am the creator of my own destiny.

1598) All of my relationships are healthy, positive, and bring only good into my life.

1599) Ambition is a blessing because it means that I will never settle for mediocrity.

1600) As a man I have been gifted with immeasurable power to change myself and others.

17

Lesson XVII. Failure

The warrior in you isn't afraid to fail - because he knows that failing is simply an opportunity to learn something new and do things better next time. He can fail many times but he doesn't make the same mistake twice.

Challenge: Allow yourself to fail and learn from it

Look at all of your mistakes from a new perspective. Some people make a name for themselves based solely on their mistakes. The most successful people in history have all had to make mistakes before they succeeded. By allowing yourself to fail, you'll be able to learn from what you did wrong and find out where your weaknesses are.

In life, it's inevitable that you will make big and small mistakes. People who succeed in life allow their mistakes to guide them and become better people.

Every mistake that you make is a lesson to help you get better at whatever it is that you're trying to do. Instead of getting discouraged by mistakes, embrace them and take ownership in everything that happens to you during your life.

No matter how hard something might seem, there's always a way around it. Even if you can't see it right now, there's always a solution to every problem.

Change your perspective to this: There are no mistakes in life, only lessons learned. By allowing yourself to fail, you'll be able to learn how to get back up and keep moving forward.

To start, make a list of activities that you'd want to perform yet aren't confident in. This can be anything from public speaking to starting a small business. Once you have your list, choose one of the activities to work on right now. By taking this step, you'll have the chance to learn something by trial and error.

It is not always necessary to have a big plan, sometimes it

is good to just go with the flow and see where it takes you. Either way, success or failure, both can teach you something about yourself as a person.

Failures are not the opposite of successes; they're part of success. By allowing yourself to make mistakes and learn from them, everything else will become much easier.

Affirmations 1601-1700

1601) Each day that passes brings me one step closer to achieving my dreams and goals.

1602) Excuses are the seeds of failure, never letting excuses grow into anything more.

1603) I am always developing my mind, body, and spirit into the best that they can be.

1604) I am grateful for everything that life has presented to me, even if good or bad.

1605) I am not afraid to be me, I put myself first that is why people love me so much.

1606) I don't need anyone else's approval to be myself, I already approve of who I am.

1607) I have strength in me no one else has and it makes me capable of doing anything.

1608) I overcame a lot of obstacles already so today is not the day for me to give up.

1609) I will not let this day be just another day, it is an opportunity for greatness.

1610) My mistakes are a learning experience that will help me reach my full potential.

1611) Obstacles may slow me down, but they will never stop me from achieving my goals.

1612) Obstacles only make me stronger because every time it gets tough, I get tougher.

1613) Success does not come to those who wait; it comes to those who work hard for it.

1614) Today will be the best day of my life because I won't take anything for granted.

1615) Today, feel the power of being a man with increased testosterone hormone levels.

1616) Today, I leave fear and doubt behind and embrace love, acceptance and gratitude.

1617) When it comes down to it, conquering obstacles is easy because I am unstoppable.

1618) All the knowledge I need is inside me now, I just need to learn how to access it.

1619) Before I make any decision today, I carefully consider the possible consequences.

1620) I am committed to setting and maintaining healthy boundaries in my relationships.

1621) I am male in all my parts and functions; masculine in mind, heart, body and soul.

1622) I am on a path of self-discovery as I am always learning new things about myself.

1623) I am the kind of person who makes things happen; I take action and I get results.

1624) I am the only one in charge of my life so I will take control and be unstoppable.

1625) I am the ruler of my own kingdom and everything that happens to me is on purpose.

1626) I can make excuses all day but they will not get me anywhere, so why even bother?

1627) I cannot control anyone's opinion of me but I can control who I am and what I do.

1628) I have a purpose for my life and I am fully committed to fulfilling that purpose.

1629) I will not let my weaknesses control me because everything in life has a purpose.

1630) It doesn't matter how long the climb is, as long as I am moving towards my goals.

1631) It is okay if I do not know everything because there is so much to learn in life.

1632) Life brings good people, situations, and opportunities into my life all the time.

1633) Life can be great if we make it great, nobody else has the power to do it but us.

1634) My vision for the future is coming together moment by moment as I pursue success.

1635) No matter how much stress life may bring me, I will find a way to manage it well.

1636) Successful people are willing to be unpopular in order to get their point across.

1637) The better I feel, the more energy I have to be successful in achieving my goals.

1638) When I find myself in a difficult situation, I will remember how far I have come.

1639) I am the most loving, generous, kind, compassionate person that I can possibly be.

1640) Each dollar that comes my way brings more opportunities for me to succeed in life.

1641) Every breath, every moment is another chance to be brave and strong and honorable.

1642) Every problem presents me with an opportunity to learn something new about myself.

1643) Everyone in life that is successful had failed at something before they succeeded.

1644) Everything in life starts with a dream and my dream is finally starting right now.

1645) Excuses show a lack in my character because winners have no excuses, only results.

1646) I am a man of my word so I will hold myself accountable for everything that I say.

1647) I am always one step ahead, looking into the future and planning how to get there.

1648) I am surrounded by like-minded people who are attracting success into their lives.

1649) I choose happiness over sadness because happiness makes tomorrow that much better.

1650) I don't care what other people think about me, I follow my own dreams and desires.

1651) I don't need to know how it's going to be; I just need to go and see what happens.

1652) I will never go back to my old ways, because I am a new person with better habits.

1653) I will not let my failures define who I am, only the future that lies ahead of me.

1654) If it's good, I want more of it. If it's bad, I now know what not to do next time.

1655) If life is going to test me, then so be it, because I have already won the battle.

1656) If something isn't working, I will find a different approach until I get it right.

1657) It's okay to open up, because I have friends who are here for me when I need them.

1658) Many people have created lasting legacies by never quitting when things got tough.

1659) No one can push me around because I have a strong mind that is ready for anything.

1660) The testosterone within me has been unleashed, and it changes everything about me.

1661) Today I am grateful for my immeasurable power to choose what I want to experience.

1662) Today is all about taking steps towards my future because tomorrow isn't promised.

1663) Today, I will choose to be kind over everything because the world needs more love.

1664) Today, the sun shines brightly on my world, making everything easy and manageable.

1665) I believe in myself and because I do, I am able to achieve great things in my life.

1666) I can handle whatever happens in my life today; I am strong enough to deal with it.

1667) I don't have time to worry about what others think of me because life is too short.

1668) I don't have to be perfect for everyone, but I do have to put my best foot forward.

1669) I will push myself to be the best that I can be and exceed everyone's expectations.

1670) It is easy for me to forgive others because I understand that we all make mistakes.

1671) It's okay if others are more successful than me, because I have faith in what I do.

1672) My past has made me the man I am today, but I will make sure my future is brighter.

1673) No matter how difficult life gets; I will always wake up the next day with a smile.

1674) Success is not a result of what happens to me, but a matter of how I respond to it.

1675) The more that I give, the more that my life will reflect positivity and prosperity.

1676) Today, I will let my dreams guide me and take action towards making them a reality.

1677) When I look back on my life, all of my experiences have led me to where I am today.

1678) Each day, I become stronger as I continue to change my world by creating new habits.

1679) Everything works out for me without any effort on my part; I choose to believe this.

1680) I am a man, an heir of the universe, a friend of nature. I am here to live out loud.

1681) I am a powerhouse of positive energy; when I walk in the room, people feel the vibe.

1682) I am an excellent person because I give so much of myself for the benefit of others.

1683) I can take care of myself and create a happy life for myself if I put my mind to it.

1684) I know that as I grow and evolve, all aspects of my life will change for the better.

1685) I only attract positive people into my life who are supportive and give me the same.

1686) I refuse to live a life filled with regret because I am always learning and growing.

1687) I will finish all my tasks today because there is nothing stopping me from doing so.

1688) I will never change for anyone because I am who I am and that's what makes me great.

1689) I will not let toxic people affect my life because they are just passing through it.

1690) I will not waste time feeling sorry for myself because there is too much work to do.

1691) I work hard and I do it for myself; I am thankful when others appreciate my efforts.

1692) If I don't know how to do something, then guess what? That means I'm about to learn.

1693) It's time to go out there and be great because nobody else is going to do it for me.

1694) My body is changing more and more each day into that of a powerful, masculine man's.

1695) My future belongs to me so I will not let anyone or anything influence my happiness.

1696) My mistakes made me wiser so today I am going to stay focused on learning from them.

1697) My past does not dictate my future because I am the only one who can make it better.

1698) Success starts in the mind because if you don't think success, it will never happen.

1699) Today is going to be a great day because I am the most positive person in the world.

1700) Today, I am going to work on being more productive so that I have more time for fun.

18

Lesson XVIII. Reward

The warrior in you doesn't expect applause - he only asks for the chance to prove himself. He knows that a job well done is its own reward, and that true satisfaction comes from within your heart and soul.

Challenge: Cultivate Self-Love

Remember, you were not put on this planet to suffer. You are a unique and magnificent creature and life is wonderful! It's time to take charge of your own happiness. This begins with loving yourself.

Loving yourself begins with taking care of yourself. Before you can love someone else, you need to learn how to love yourself first.

Self-love is the most powerful thing that you will ever experience with your entire being. By loving yourself with all of your heart and soul, it will allow you to do anything in the world.

If there is one lesson about self-love that you should take from this book, it's the lesson of knowing how to forgive yourself. Everything that has ever happened to you is an experience and those experiences have taught us so much about life.

Learn from every mistake that you've made in your life because from those mistakes comes wisdom. Allow your heart to forgive your soul for all of the things that you've done wrong. Once you do this, your life will open up to new possibilities and opportunities.

When it comes down to it, loving yourself is like a muscle: The more you work on strengthening it, the better and stronger it will become. It may seem daunting at first; however, know that you can do it.

No matter how much you try to make excuses for yourself, know that there are no valid reasons why you should not love yourself today. You are worthy of everything in the world, so make sure that you start treating yourself better starting now!

How do you know if you are on the right path? Accept compliments graciously without deflecting them or diminishing their worth. If you feel like you do not deserve them, try to withstand your reflex to deflect the praise. Later you should contemplate this for a moment and ask yourself why you do not feel that you deserve the praise.

Affirmations 1701-1800

1701) When someone is unkind to me, it only serves as motivation for me to improve myself.

1702) Decisions are made by those who show up, so today I am making the best decision ever.

1703) Every day I practice being more optimistic so one day it won't be a practice anymore.

1704) Every day in every way, I'm getting better and better. All my dreams are coming true.

1705) Every morning when I wake up, I will think about how lucky I am before anything else.

1706) Everything that I am going through right now will shape me into who I am meant to be.

1707) Everything that I have gone through so far has prepared me for what is about to come.

1708) I am a calm and patient person who stands in my power without getting angry or upset.

1709) I am not afraid of failure because it is a necessary step for my growth and learning.

1710) I am not afraid to fail because I know that each failure brings me closer to success.

1711) I am now breathing richer air filled with more oxygen than I've ever breathed before.

1712) I command my mind to focus with laser-like intensity on what is most important to me.

1713) I easily create prosperity in my life through intelligent decisions and wise actions.

1714) I make my own destiny, never letting what others do get in the way of me being great.

1715) I will always fight for my health because there are too many people who depend on me.

1716) I will not be ashamed of the past, because it has made me into the person I am today.

1717) If I believe that I can do something, then there is no stopping me from achieving it.

1718) It does not matter how long it takes, because the end result will always be worth it.

1719) It's never too late to do what needs to be done so there is no time like the present.

1720) My life is full of promises so today is the day that every single promise comes true.

1721) No matter how many times life knocks me down, I am always quick to get back up again.

1722) No matter what they say about me, I know I'm awesome inside even if nobody else does.

1723) Obstacles may slow me down, but they will never stop me from going after what I want.

1724) The greatest pleasure in life is doing for others what they cannot do for themselves.

1725) The only person stopping me from being successful is myself, nobody else can stop me.

1726) Today I will stay positive, even when everything seems to be falling apart around me.

1727) Today is a new day, so it's okay if I don't accomplish everything that I had planned.

1728) Today is going to be a stepping stone in my life that will help me overcome anything.

1729) I allow other people's thoughts to come into my mind without accepting them as my own.

1730) I am a man of honor; therefore, I will do everything that is right and expected of me.

1731) I am a man on a mission who is willing to do whatever it takes to accomplish my goals.

1732) I am thankful for all of my mentors because they have helped me become who I am today.

1733) It is not my past that defines who I am, but it's how I choose to live in the present.

1734) My body is my home and I treat it as such by keeping it healthy, clean, and nourished.

1735) My past does not have to define me because I am more than just a result of my choices.

1736) My thoughts are in perfect alignment with who I am and what I want most in this world.

1737) Success is my right and it's on its way because nothing can stop me from achieving it.

1738) The challenge of earning money teaches me new skills and helps me to grow as a person.

1739) The money that I need comes to me easily and effortlessly, always at the perfect time.

1740) All I need to know is inside of me now; I don't need anybody else's approval or advice.

1741) Each day brings new opportunities for me to achieve greatness in every area of my life.

1742) Every day that I spend helping others grow and improve their lives is a success for me.

1743) I am not afraid of anything because I know everything is going to work out in my favor.

1744) I am willing to trust the process because everything will work out for my highest good.

1745) I have all of the tools I need inside myself to be successful; I just need to use them.

1746) I have only one life to live, so today I will do things that make me happy and excited.

1747) I will not let anyone else's negativity bring me down, only positivity can bring me up.

1748) I will put as much love into this world as possible because that is what life deserves.

1749) If you want something, go out there and get it because nothing comes without hard work.

1750) Inner peace comes from within so every single day of my life must be peaceful and calm.

1751) My mind is more powerful than anything else; it's up to me what I choose to do with it.

1752) My passion for my goals, is far greater than any fear or obstacle that may come my way.

1753) My sex expression is natural, honest, and wholesome. It arouses respect and admiration.

1754) My thoughts influence my actions so today I will think positively before anything else.

1755) No matter what happens in life, I will always believe that there is good coming my way.

1756) The mind is everything so today, my brain is going to take me further than ever before.

1757) The world is mine to do with whatever I please because I know who I am and what I want.

1758) Today is all about moving towards my future so today must be outstanding and legendary.

1759) Today, I am a better person than yesterday and tomorrow will be even better than today.

1760) With each passing day I become stronger, more commanding, more confident and sexier.

1761) Every moment of my life is a new beginning but I am thankful for where I have come from.

1762) Everything that happens in my life has a purpose so today I will search for its meaning.

1763) Excuses are for losers but winners use obstacles as fuel to push themselves even harder.

1764) I always choose my words carefully, no one can take my power away with their mind games.

1765) I am capable of accomplishing anything because I am driven by passion more than by fear.

1766) I am committed to taking care of myself and treating my body like the temple that it is.

1767) I have the courage to move forward with my life no matter what obstacles are in my path.

1768) I make time for myself because if I don't take care of myself, I can't help anyone else.

1769) I speak and think in positive ways, and attract positive people and circumstances to me.

1770) I thank myself every day for the people, things and opportunities that I have in my life.

1771) If someone betrays me, then so be it because karma does not discriminate against anyone.

1772) If you want something, don't wait for it to come to you. Go out there and make it yours.

1773) My beliefs about money are creating my financial reality faster than the speed of light.

1774) The stronger, smarter and more experienced that I become, the more successful I will be.

1775) Today and every day, I choose positivity. No matter how hard it gets, I'm not giving up.

1776) Today is a great day to live life the way I choose and not how anyone else wants me too.

1777) Today nothing can stop me from thinking positive and staying positive throughout my day.

1778) Today, I am grateful for everything in my life as it has brought me to where I am today.

1779) Where there's a will, there's always a way so I am always full of ways to be successful.

1780) All the knowledge that I need is already inside of me. Now it's time for me to access it.

1781) Even when people push me down or laugh at me, I will keep my head up and remain positive.

1782) Every day that I give thanks for all the good in my life, more blessings come back to me.

1783) Every day I become stronger and wiser because I pride myself on learning from my mistakes.

1784) Growth happens when we leave our comfort zone and go beyond what we thought was possible.

1785) I am grateful for the little things, because it teaches me to be grateful for everything.

1786) I don't need to worry about what others think of me because their opinions are not facts.

1787) I have an amazing sense of humor that makes me who I am today, no one could ask for more.

1788) I now embrace my failures as well as my successes, learning something valuable from both.

1789) I surround myself with other energetic, enthusiastic people who bring out the best in me.

1790) I will always do my best to be a good person because I know life is about helping others.

1791) If you can dream it, then you can do it… take that leap of faith and live the impossible.

1792) In order to be successful, I must first believe that I am the one destined for greatness.

1793) I've got this. I am confident in my abilities to be successful in everything I do today.

1794) Life isn't about waiting for the storm to pass, it's about learning to dance in the rain.

1795) Mistakes are perfectly imperfect because they allow us to learn something new every time.

1796) My mind is rich with creative ideas for making my life even more successful and abundant.

1797) My past is just a story that mustn't be told again, but my future is still being written.

1798) My success starts with me; I create it every day by the thoughts that I put into my mind.

1799) Obstacles will never defeat me because I overcome them every time they appear in my life.

1800) The key to success in any area of life is to focus my mind on solutions, not on problems.

19

Lesson XIX. Love

The warrior in you isn't afraid to say "I love you" - even when it means taking a risk. He knows that when he says "I love you," the other person gets a chance to run away, but only if they're not feeling the same thing. If his words make someone else feel something special, he can be thankful for the chance to open his heart and express the love that's in it.

Challenge: Compliment other people

When you start complimenting other people, it will actually help you to become much more confident in yourself. When you see someone else achieve success, or accomplish something amazing, tell them how much you respect their progress.

If you feel like a certain person is putting themselves down too often, do your best to compliment them on a specific trait. Whenever possible, try to build other people up, rather than tearing them down.

If you wish to be the best version of yourself that you can possibly be, then you need to surround yourself with other positive people. Encourage the people you care about to grow in life and follow their pursuits. Having positive people around you is the best way to ensure that you will stay on the right path to becoming successful.

Today, make a point to compliment at least three other people. You do not have to go out of your way to find someone who deserves it; simply look around.

Doing things that make other people happy, even something so small as a compliment, will have a positive impact on your life. Not only this, but it will also help to cultivate a sense of community within the people around you and create new opportunities for them to succeed.

Affirmations 1801-1900

1801) The more money that comes into my life, the more freedom I have to do what matters to me.

1802) With each new day, comes a new opportunity to get better at something that matters to me.

1803) Every day is a new adventure where I am able to explore and discover who I am meant to be.

1804) Everything that happens brings me one step closer to achieving all of my dreams and goals.

1805) I am capable of anything and everything that I put my mind to, I just need to get it done.

1806) I am excited about whatever may happen next in my life as long as it is something amazing.

1807) I am filled with inspiration as I allow the divine order of the universe to direct me now.

1808) I am the author of my own destiny so today I accept another opportunity to live life well.

1809) I am unique and talented; my talent is one-of-a-kind and cannot be matched by anyone else.

1810) I create a healthy financial pattern in my life so I have the freedom to pursue my dreams.

1811) I walk with confidence in everything I do because I know who I am and what I'm capable of.

1812) I welcome change because it is one of the main ingredients to a happy and fulfilling life.

1813) I will stop comparing myself to everyone else because it is impossible to be someone else.

1814) My decisions are based on good judgment which will only lead to more opportunities for me.

1815) No matter what, everything is going to work out in my favor because I will make it happen.

1816) The law of attraction ensures that my life will always be filled with wonderful surprises.

1817) Today I choose to be the author of all my own thoughts, behaviors, attitudes and emotions.

1818) Today is going to be amazing no matter what happens because by saying that, it becomes so.

1819) As long as my intentions are pure and positive, nothing can stop me from achieving success.

1820) I expect great things when I think about them. It's important that I believe it can happen.

1821) I focus my attention on the present, where life happens and things come together with ease.

1822) I know there is a reason I am still here today, and it's up to me to find out what that is.

1823) I know who I am and I like knowing that people can rely on me if they need help or support.

1824) I will never let life knock me down because I am a fighter and winners fight until the end.

1825) If I am feeling sad, then all I need to do is change my thoughts and I'll feel happy again.

1826) If you believe in something, don't ever give up on it because your faith makes it possible.

1827) Just when I think things are getting hard, it means that they are about to get much better.

1828) My happiness depends on how well I look after myself physically, mentally, and emotionally.

1829) No matter what the problem, there is a solution so I will never lose faith or give up hope.

1830) No one can ever stop me from achieving my dreams and it doesn't matter what they try to do.

1831) The more obstacles that show up in my life now, the bigger success I will achieve later on.

1832) The only person that I should live up to, is the unique and wonderful individual that I am.

1833) The past cannot be changed but the future can be shaped by my present thoughts and actions.

1834) Even when times are tough, there is always something good that comes out of every situation.

1835) Every single day in life can be a new beginning so today better than most for making change.

1836) Every single thing that has happened in my life thus far has been preparing me for the best.

1837) I create positive and successful habits and stick with them until they become natural to me.

1838) If not me, who? If not now, when? Success waits for no one so it's time to make mine happen.

1839) My dream is written on my heart and it is only a matter of time before the dream comes true.

1840) My thoughts and actions must always be in sync to ensure that I live my life to the fullest.

1841) My thoughts are always positive about my future because I know that the best is yet to come.

1842) The higher the risk, the greater the reward so why would I want safe instead of spectacular?

1843) Today, I choose to see the positive side of all things and never stop looking for solutions.

1844) When I think about what I want, my mind automatically goes to work for me to make it happen.

1845) Wherever I focus my thoughts is where I place my energy, and that will always be on success.

1846) Who controls my thoughts? I do. I control my thoughts to build myself up, not break me down.

1847) A new day brings with it a new opportunity to have a positive impact on somebody else's life.

1848) All of the tools that I need are already inside me. Now it's time for me to begin using them.

1849) As long as I remember where it all began, there is nothing that can stop me from being great.

1850) Doing the best I can every day is all that really matters. the rest will take care of itself.

1851) Every day, I do my best to live in the present moment because all good things come from here.

1852) I am driven by my own ambitions and desires; I do not compare myself to other people anymore.

1853) I have the strength and courage to do things that scare me because I have been through worse.

1854) I make mistakes, but I always move forward with a greater understanding of myself and others.

1855) If today were my last day on earth, would I be happy about how things turned out? Absolutely.

1856) If you want something, you have to do something because life isn't going to just give it you.

1857) It is not about lack of opportunity that holds me back, it is my limitations holding me back.

1858) Just when the caterpillar thought the world was ending, he turned into a beautiful butterfly.

1859) Being positive is a choice I have made every day because I want to see the good in all things.

1860) I am a magnet to wealth and abundance, and that is why I deserve nothing but the best in life.

1861) I am going to live today as if it were my last because I have no idea when tomorrow will come.

1862) I am thankful for today's mistakes because they are the stepping stones of tomorrow's success.

1863) I realize the importance of leading my life on my terms; no one gets to make decisions for me.

1864) I will not let my future be determined by worry and fear because nothing good comes out of it.

1865) If I get frustrated, I take a deep breath and relax. Then, I focus on what matters most to me.

1866) If someone makes a negative comment about me, I will use it as motivation to prove them wrong.

1867) It's okay if I don't know what to do, because I know that something good is around the corner.

1868) My future is waiting for me and it is more beautiful than anything I could have ever imagined.

1869) My masculinity is not a curse but a gift which grants me immeasurable power and opportunities.

1870) My past is perfect because it brought me to this present moment exactly as it was meant to be.

1871) No matter how many times I fail, that doesn't mean that I don't have what it takes to succeed.

1872) No one can change who I am without my permission, so today I am claiming ownership of my life.

1873) Nothing is permanent in life except for my commitment to succeed and achieve all of my dreams.

1874) Successful people make mistakes. The difference between them and me is they don't dwell on it.

1875) The frequency of my mind is improving daily because I practice positive thinking all the time.

1876) The more I overcome challenges in my life, the stronger I get and the bigger rewards await me.

1877) The only thing holding me back is myself because I am the one who puts limitations on my life.

1878) When it seems like no one is there for me, I know that the angels are always watching over me.

1879) Even though there may be hard times in life, I know that things are always going to get better.

1880) Every mistake I've made has been an opportunity to learn something new about myself and others.

1881) I choose to see the positive in all situations even though it may not be there at first glance.

1882) I have an overflowing abundance of prosperity, success, wealth, health and wellness in my life.

1883) I refuse to dwell on the things that I cannot change, yesterday is gone and today is a new day.

1884) I will not let my past define who I am because today I choose the person that I want to become.

1885) It doesn't matter if people try to hold me back-what matters is that I continue moving forward.

1886) My destiny is in my hands and I will not allow anything or anyone to distract me from my goals.

1887) My fears can hold me back or push me to the edge, but it is up to me which direction they take.

1888) My purpose in life is to be the best that I can be and I will not stop until I achieve my goal.

1889) The bigger picture guides me through this journey called life; it's not easy but it's worth it.

1890) The future is waiting for me right around the corner so I will cherish every moment until then.

1891) The world is a beautiful place that constantly gives and gives and I will be sure to give back.

1892) Today, I choose to see the good in all things and appreciate even the smallest of life's gifts.

1893) Today, I will remain focused on achieving my goals no matter how many distractions come my way.

1894) When opportunities arise that could help me achieve success, I embrace them without hesitation.

1895) Each day is an opportunity for me to shine as long as I stay positive and put in my best effort.

1896) Each day, I do my best to become a better version of myself than the one that existed yesterday.

1897) Every challenge builds my strength and endurance so I can handle anything that is thrown my way.

1898) Every mistake is an opportunity to learn, so I will take my mistakes and turn them into lessons.

1899) I am grateful for everything that life has given to me even though it does not seem like enough.

1900) I focus only on the positive thoughts every day because they shape who I am into someone better.

20

Lesson XX. Protection

The warrior in you doesn't need to fight everyone he sees - but, when he needs to defend himself or someone else, he'll do it without thinking twice. He knows this life is too short for hatred and bitterness and wants to be able to look back on his life without any regrets. He wants to be the kind of person who people can rely on when things get out of control, not someone who makes it worse with curses and threats.

Challenge: Stay calm and grounded

You will always run into other people who push your buttons and try to get a reaction out of you. Some people live for drama and this actually makes them feel more alive. These types of people tend to be unpleasant to be around and very draining on the energy of those that they come across.

If someone is trying to get a rise out of you, do not give them the satisfaction. People with confidence and strong values are calm and collected; they rarely lose their temper and even when they do, it's always for a good reason and under extreme circumstances.

Do your best to remain positive and never let another person bring you down with their negative energy. It is also good to be straightforward with people who try to provoke you. Express your concerns to them in a civil manner and let them know that their behavior is affecting you.

Even if they refuse to change their ways, by expressing what bothers you without letting your emotions get the better of you, you will feel much more at peace because you were mature enough to handle the situation.

If someone challenges one of your values, simply let them know that this is a topic that you do not want to discuss. If they continue to challenge your values, simply walk away from them and let their lack of respect go unacknowledged.

To be successful in life, you need to have self-respect that is not contingent on the opinions of others. Having confidence in yourself will prevent any toxic people from draining you of your positive attitude.

Affirmations 1901-2000

1901) I will not give in to the temptation of negativity because positivity reigns supreme in my life.

1902) If I really want something, why would I let something as trivial as a little discomfort stop me?

1903) My decisions are based on good judgment to ensure that they are always beneficial for my future.

1904) No matter what problems I face, I always bounce back up and keep pushing forward with my dreams.

1905) People who don't appreciate what they have simply aren't grateful enough-it's as simple as that.

1906) The limits that other people place on me don't exist in reality; they only exist in their minds.

1907) The power to succeed is within me so I will not allow anything to stop me from being successful.

1908) The world needs people like me, who are willing to take on the responsibility of helping others.

1909) Today my thoughts are filled with reasons why things are getting better in all areas of my life.

1910) When failure knocks on my door, I always open it without fear because that's how success enters.

1911) All of my needs are met abundantly by an infinite source of supply, which is available to me now.

1912) I am not afraid of what life throws at me, because I have been through worse and came out on top.

1913) I am the master of my own destiny and it is my desire to help others achieve their goals in life.

1914) I choose to be happy by focusing on what is right about my life instead of what is wrong with it.

1915) I need to take control because everything I want in life starts with me taking a step towards it.

1916) I only attract the best of people into my life, and that is why everything in my life is amazing.

1917) I refuse to be controlled by society's definition of who I am because this is my life not theirs.

1918) I will never stop trying to accomplish all of my dreams because starting today, I am unstoppable.

1919) I will not let fear stop me from taking risks but instead show courage in the face of challenges.

1920) The more successful and grateful I become; the more reasons people will find to be jealous of me.

1921) The only person who can limit my potential is me so today, I set out to accomplish something big.

1922) Today is the day that all of my dreams come true so bring on anything that wants to challenge me.

1923) Today, I feel good about myself because my thoughts are all filled with positivity and happiness.

1924) Every single moment brings a new opportunity and a blessing from above… it's time to embrace them.

1925) I am always learning from my mistakes because this gives me an opportunity to become a better man.

1926) I refuse to let anyone else define success for me because my success is defined by how happy I am.

1927) My actions, thoughts and emotions support the positive development of my life and those around me.

1928) Today isn't just another day, it's a new opportunity to start over and create a life worth living.

1929) As long as I stay focused on my goals and keep moving forward, nothing can ever truly hold me back.

1930) At this very moment, everything is okay; if anything changes, I will be ready to face them head-on.

1931) Every single person deserves happiness. So, focusing on how good others have it in comparison with how bad I may have it will never bring anything but self-pity into my life.

1932) My future is forming each and every day, and I am excited to see where my positive choices lead me.

1933) My masculine energy is guiding me into my rightful place as a strong, successful leader in society.

1934) My thoughts are powerful and positive. My mind is focused on what needs to be done, not on failure.

1935) Sometimes it's best for me to put my feelings aside so I don't do anything I might regret later on.

1936) I am perfectly balanced in all areas of my life - physically, mentally, emotionally and spiritually.

1937) I easily understand how thoughts become things, and manifest my desires using the power of my words.

1938) Even if there are obstacles in my path, I will not be stopped because I am on the path of greatness.

1939) Even though the world around me may change, my attitude cannot because there is too much work to do.

1940) I am able to show affection and love, while maintaining healthy boundaries with everyone in my life.

1941) I know that my life is full of amazing opportunities because my life is full of amazing experiences.

1942) If something is bothering me, all I have to do is change my perception on it and everything changes.

1943) I'm smart enough, strong enough and good looking enough to be just about anywhere that I want to be.

1944) My success is not determined by how much money I make but rather how happy I make other people feel.

1945) Success in every area of life comes from having a positive attitude and knowing that it is possible.

1946) To be successful today, I will do what successful people do even if that means doing it differently.

1947) Today, I am determined to be positive and optimistic no matter how hard life tries to bring me down.

1948) Whatever happens today is meant to happen so it's all up to me to learn from the situation and grow.

1949) When it seems like everyone is against you, this only means that something great is about to happen.

1950) I am grateful for what I have. This feeling of gratitude brings more prosperity to my life every day.

1951) I am hardworking and willing to go the extra mile because that's what has made me successful in life.

1952) If you dream of something, chase that dream no matter how impossible it seems because it is possible.

1953) It is not what others say about me that counts, it is how I feel about myself and my accomplishments.

1954) It's not what happens to me but how I choose to see it that matters most so today I choose happiness.

1955) The more focused on the present moment I am, the more opportunities for success and happiness I have.

1956) When the going gets rough, the rough get going and nothing is going to stop me from being successful.

1957) When times become tough, all I need to do is remember who I am and everything becomes possible again.

1958) All of my wishes will come true if I wish for positivity because negative things will not come my way.

1959) Every morning when I wake up, even if nothing good has happened yet, I know today will still be great.

1960) I am grateful for the fears that have stopped me in the past, because they are now making me stronger.

1961) I am grateful to be alive today; I'm successful because I wake up every morning with a reason to live.

1962) I am not afraid of anything; failure is an opportunity to learn and success is an opportunity to grow.

1963) I have a good sense of humor. It keeps me optimistic and helps me to understand people so much better.

1964) I have the courage to go out into this world because I know that life is worth living to its fullest.

1965) I will not be discouraged by the failures of yesterday, because today is a new opportunity to succeed.

1966) Life is on my side. Because everything in the world works in my favor, all of my goals are achievable.

1967) My life may not be perfect but I am willing to do what it takes for it to become as close as possible.

1968) People are always following me but not because I am a follower myself but because I set the standards.

1969) Right now is the perfect time for me to take action and do something that will change my life forever.

1970) The more I let go of what happened in my past, the better chance I have at creating an amazing future.

1971) Worrying about bad things happening will only make them come true so no more negative thoughts for me.

1972) Each day, I become more organized as it helps me accomplish all of my goals faster with higher quality.

1973) Even when it feels like no one cares, I know deep down that there are people that I can really rely on.

1974) I am a man who is responsible for his own actions and no amount of rationalizing will change that fact.

1975) I have achieved everything I have ever wanted and everything that comes next will be even more amazing.

1976) If you want something, all you have to do is go out and get it because nothing comes without hard work.

1977) My body deserves self-care; too often I neglect it which leads to feeling tired, stressed, and unhappy.

1978) My voice matters; if no one hears it, that's okay because what matters is that I know I said something.

1979) Now is the time to make things happen, to pull out all the stops, go for what I really want and get it.

1980) Successful people do not worry about pleasing other people; they worry about achieving their own goals.

1981) There is nothing that can stop me except myself, so I will not let my fear get in the way of my dreams.

1982) To love myself unconditionally gives me permission to walk through this beautiful journey we call life.

1983) When I feel small, I remember that there are bigger things in this world than me and I am a part of it.

1984) Each day brings with it a fresh new canvas for me to create an inspiring painting that is uniquely mine.

1985) I am a man of action as I am always doing something to improve my life and the lives of those around me.

1986) It does not matter who likes me or who does not because they are judging me based on their own problems.

1987) My thoughts create feelings which cause positive actions that result in prosperity and abundance for me.

1988) The more I can see people for who they really are, the less I have to worry about what they think of me.

1989) There is nothing in this world that can stop me from achieving anything if it is something I truly want.

1990) When times are hard, all I need to do is take one day at a time and before long I'll turn things around.

1991) Doubts and fears will try to creep into my mind, but they always lose against my focus and determination.

1992) Every day brings with it a fresh new canvas for me to create an inspiring painting that is uniquely mine.

1993) I will always speak words of encouragement to other people because I know it can make all the difference.

1994) Today will be full of positive experiences as long as I go after what matters to me with all of my heart.

1995) When life throws lemons at me, all I have to do is smile because it's a sign that I am about to be great.

1996) I am confident in myself because I know that life has given me all the tools that I need to be successful.

1997) I am most happy when I find new opportunities to grow as an individual because this is my purpose in life.

1998) I am not going to let anyone else's doubts and fears become my own because there is no reason they should.

1999) I am thankful for the lessons that life has taught me because they are what keeps leading me to happiness.

2000) I am the calm in the center of the storm. Nothing can get to me because I am strong on the inside and out.

21

Lesson XXI. Respect

The warrior in you won't tolerate emotional or physical abuse - because he knows that respect is a two-way street. He never abuses his power or mistreats people who are weaker than him, especially children.

Challenge: Diminish negative influences

Every person that you surround yourself with will have a huge impact on your life. Toxic people will leave a lasting, negative impression on you and this can make it very difficult to get back onto the right path.

The best way to avoid negative influences is by surrounding yourself with positive people who are going to help push you in the right direction. We are the sum of the people that we spend the most time with, so you need to be very selective about who you let into your life. However, some people are just not easy to be around, no matter how many positive influences you have around yourself.

Not only this, but some individuals might not even realize that their words and actions are affecting other people in a negative way. If you come across someone who is bringing you down with them, try to let go of the situation because sometimes it just isn't worth it to be affected by negativity.

Forgiveness will only make the situation worse. You need to cut your ties with toxic people. If you are close to them, it may be difficult to do this because of the effort that they have put into your relationship. However, if you continue to allow people who bring nothing but negativity into your life, then you will never truly find happiness within yourself.

When you have no one in existence that brings you joy, you will begin to resent the world around you. No matter how strong your willpower is, toxic people can still find their way into your life and leave their mark of misery that simply cannot be washed away with simple apologies.

Removing negative influences from your life can be a freeing experience as long as it is done for the right reasons. Remember, there are plenty of people in the world who can have a positive influence on you so don't let toxic personalities ruin your life.

Affirmations 2001-2100

2001) I release all thoughts of fear, doubt and worry from my mind knowing that these things no longer serve me.

2002) If someone doesn't want to see you succeed then don't worry about it because they are just jealous of you.

2003) My actions are always lined up with my goals because I am doing what will get me closer to achieving them.

2004) Successful people don't wait for their ship to come in, they build a boat and create a sea for themselves.

2005) The remarkable thing about me is that no matter how hard times may be, I always find a way to smile again.

2006) Today, my thoughts are powerful and positive. My mind is focused on what needs to be done, not on failure.

2007) When I was a child, I couldn't control my environment but as an adult, I am the master of every situation.

2008) I am strong on the inside and out because my mind is healthy and I know that my thoughts create my reality.

2009) I have so much to look forward to in this life because I am constantly growing into the best that I can be.

2010) I have the tenacity to follow through with any project until it is completed - no matter how long it takes.

2011) I know what it means to appreciate life because there are many who has not lived to see the sun rise again.

2012) I now recognize that the only limits to the possibilities in my life are those that I place on them myself.

2013) Just because someone thinks something can't be done doesn't mean it can't. all it means is that they won't.

2014) My life does not depend on how much money I make, but rather the difference I make in other people's lives.

2015) Every day, I do my best to make the world a little bit better as I know that this is what life is all about.

2016) Every single person who I come across today will lift me up and inspire me to be the best version of myself.

2017) I can achieve anything that I set out to accomplish because I am a man of high self-esteem and self-respect.

2018) I let go of my past mistakes. I forgive myself for all that has happened, and I focus on today's blessings.

2019) It doesn't matter how many people doubt me; I will always follow my heart because it knows what it is doing.

2020) My life is full of endless possibilities so today I will focus on the possibilities and not the limitations.

2021) The more I focus on my strengths and abilities, the easier it becomes to overcome my fears and insecurities.

2022) There is nothing that can get in the way of me fulfilling my destiny because it has already been determined.

2023) Whether or not my past has been good or bad, it has shaped me into who I am today so it is still a blessing.

2024) Breathing in, I'm calm. Breathing out, I smile. Regardless of what happens around me, I am always in control.

2025) Every day is another chance at success and happiness because the world around me has plenty of them to offer.

2026) I am developing a wonderful character, one that is straightforward and sincere with others as well as myself.

2027) I am grateful for all the mistakes that I have made because they are what helped me to become who I am today.

2028) I am not afraid of anything anymore because every reason to be fearful has already been removed from my life.

2029) If it's not difficult there is no challenge in life worth having. Defeat is only possible if you stop trying.

2030) Look at every situation from a different angle, the only way things can get better is if we make them better.

2031) Only good things happen when I set out to achieve something. Every day is a great day for doing great things.

2032) Today is a new day that brings with it an endless supply of positive energy, opportunities and possibilities.

2033) I am a man who is driven by passion and purpose in life which means I always find a way to make things happen.

2034) I used to doubt myself, but all that has changed now because no matter what happens, I always push through it.

2035) It doesn't matter how far away your dreams are, all that matters is that you stay on the journey towards them.

2036) Successful people make the best of the time they are given. I am becoming more and more successful every day.

2037) I believe that positive thinking creates a positive reality where I am able to achieve great things in my life.

2038) I choose to live a successful and abundant life. But more than anything, I enjoy the success and the abundance.

2039) I love who I am even if nobody else does because that is exactly what will keep me going when nothing else can.

2040) I will change my thoughts and feelings about the past because it has shaped me into the person that I am today.

2041) It doesn't matter what people think about me-all that really matters is what I can do for myself and my family.

2042) When people do not want to be around me, it's because they are not yet ready for the best that I have to offer.

2043) Everything that happens to me today has the power to make me even more energetically happy than I was yesterday.

2044) Every time I give up, I'm giving control of my life to someone else and that is not something I'm interested in.

2045) I am a man who isn't afraid to put in the necessary work because I know that one day, my hard work will pay off.

2046) My success is growing by leaps and bounds each day, as I continue to succeed at making the right choices for me.

2047) Today is filled with positive energy that flows throughout every aspect of my life as an abundant, powerful man.

2048) Today, is the first day of the rest of my life which means that there is a lot left for me to do and experience.

2049) I act with confidence in everything that I do because I know that when you act confident, others will see it too.

2050) I let go of all thoughts about what others think of me. Instead, I focus on how much I love and approve of myself.

2051) If you want something, do everything in your power to get it and I will do everything in my power to get success.

2052) Let truth be my guide today while choosing thoughts, words, actions & reactions of every kind throughout the day.

2053) My mind isn't quiet, but it's not loud either; like a still pond on a windless day - clear and open for guidance.

2054) People think they can bring me down but I'm simply made of stronger stuff than that so they don't stand a chance.

2055) Thinking positively does not mean that bad things won't happen; it just means overcoming them with good thoughts.

2056) Every single time somebody judges me, they are actually showing themselves up more than they are criticizing me.

2057) Each day, my faith in myself grows stronger because I am getting better at understanding the power of my thoughts.

2058) Every day is an opportunity for me to turn over a new leaf so now seems like the perfect time for doing just that.

2059) I can create miracles. I know that anything is possible if you are willing to put in the work required to succeed.

2060) I embrace change and know that it is what has allowed me to grow into a better version of myself than ever before.

2061) If someone wants to be happy, all they have to do is choose happiness and their life will never be the same again.

2062) Life is offering me new opportunities every day with the purpose of helping me grow to a better version of myself.

2063) The people who never believe in themselves are the same people who love to tell everyone else what they cannot do.

2064) Winners are not people who never fail, they are the people who rise up after failing and do what needs to be done.

2065) All that matters is what's on the inside, not outside because the world is just a reflection of our own perception.

2066) Even if I have made mistakes, I have also learned so many things from them which means they are no longer mistakes.

2067) I love boundaries because they help me feel safe and secure, allowing both me and other people to feel comfortable.

2068) My past is the foundation of what has allowed me to become successful; I do not overlook it or take it for granted.

2069) There are always two ways to look at a situation: either as a victim or as a champion so today I choose the latter.

2070) When I make a mistake, I let go of it immediately and move forward because dwelling on the past only holds me back.

2071) If I don't trust myself, why should anyone else? There's no reason whatsoever for me not to believe in my abilities.

2072) It's okay to feel scared or nervous because these feelings remind me of how far I have come to get where I am today.

2073) Each day holds new blessings for me to receive with open arms because I know how to recognize them when they show up.

2074) If someone is talking trash about me, it's because they're just jealous of who I am and what I have going for myself.

2075) Money is a form of energy that flows to and through me at all times. Money is good; I am good; And the world is good.

2076) No matter what problems come my way; I will overcome them with ease if I know deep inside that they cannot get to me.

2077) Successful people surround themselves with other success; unsuccessful people surround themselves with other failure.

2078) Today is going to be an amazing day because I'm committed to never giving up on myself even if nobody else ever does.

2079) It doesn't matter how many times people try to knock me down; the only thing that matters is that I get back up again.

2080) My life has purpose and meaning, and every morning when I open my eyes it's another chance to live up to my potential.

2081) Today will be better than yesterday because my positive thoughts are always focused on improving my life for tomorrow.

2082) What will happen in the next moment depends on what I do right now, so I always act in the most positive way possible.

2083) Even when faced with adversity, I will remain calm and patient because I know that it is required of me to stay strong.

2084) No matter how many mistakes or setbacks or delays, we must not let anything get in the way of our progress and success.

2085) Regardless of how many times things haven't gone the way I wanted; this doesn't make me a failure-it makes me stronger.

2086) Today is my opportunity to make a fresh start by making positive changes with everything from my thinking to my actions.

2087) If I want to change my life, then the only person who needs to change is me and not anyone or anything outside of myself.

2088) People who try to bring me down do not deserve my time or attention so let them be consumed by their own darker thoughts.

2089) The more mistakes I make while learning something new, the better chance there is that success is just around the corner.

2090) People who are too negative cannot expect good things to happen to them in life, positive results require positive energy.

2091) Being an achiever is part of who I am. My achievements are a source of pride for me and they inspire others to do the same.

2092) Every day of my life can be beautiful if I choose for it to be by taking care of myself no matter what my circumstances are.

2093) My life is full of happiness, love and joy because I understand that these are the life experiences that I am meant to have.

2094) My thoughts deeply resonate with positive emotions which keep me feeling good about myself, others, and the world around me.

2095) A new day brings with it endless opportunities to take on challenges and show just how capable I am of doing so successfully.

2096) Every single action creates an equal and opposite reaction which means that any action that is taken will have a consequence.

2097) Every time I push through fear and take action, it gets easier to do what's right even if it still scares the hell out of me.

2098) My spirit of purpose infuses my mind and body with the energy I need to live life fully and accomplish what needs to be done.

2099) When life deals me a difficult hand, I take a deep breath and choose to create the best possible outcome with that situation.

2100) I do not fail because life is unfair, I fail to see opportunities coming my way which are only possible if I look hard enough.

22

Lesson XXII. Strength

The warrior in you has no problem being challenged by critics - it's better than being a coward and living an empty life. He knows that being vulnerable is a sign of strength, not weakness. And the truth is that sometimes, you can only get better when you face the most difficult of challenges.

Challenge: Be vulnerable and share your authentic feelings

Vulnerability is not synonymous with weakness; instead, it entails risking showing your real feelings to people you care about. Having the courage to be vulnerable allows you to connect with others on a deeper level and this can provide you with many opportunities that were previously closed off to you.

Many people are not comfortable with vulnerability and it is one of the main causes behind their unauthentic behavior. People who are not authentic will always be unhappy because they cannot relate to others and thus, feel very isolated.

It is important for everyone in life to find at least one person that you can be completely open and honest with. However, this does not mean that you share every thought that pops into your head with this individual; it simply means that you trust them with your feelings.

If you open yourself up to another person, they will always have the opportunity to run away from you. But what do you prefer? A life alone where you will never be hurt emotionally or a life where you are willing to put yourself out there and risk getting hurt? Do you want to have relationships with people who that are built upon superficiality or relationships that are deep and meaningful?

Without risk there will be no reward. While being vulnerable will leave you open to rejection, the experiences that are gained from it are worth it. If people do not appreciate you for who you are, then they are not good for your life.

Affirmations 2101-2200

2101) I now release all limiting thoughts about the type of person I used to be, knowing that my past does not equal who I am today.

2102) Anytime I'm feeling miserable, it's only because of a mindset that says misery is natural when all it really is just a mindset.

2103) The energy around me always makes a big impact on everything else so why even bother trying to pretend like nothing's going on?

2104) Everything in my life works in my favor, so I always have a reason to be happy and smiling no matter what is going on around me.

2105) I am a man of my word which means I will back up what I say because if I am confident in myself, then why would anyone doubt me?

2106) If someone does something to hurt me, it's only an opportunity for me to get better at choosing friends who are more supportive.

2107) When life gets tough, all it means is that I have opportunities to push myself further than ever before so why would I complain?

2108) I release all judgment of other people based on their past or current actions knowing that everyone is on their own life journey.

2109) I release all limiting thoughts about what others expect me to do with my life. Instead, I focus on what I want to do with my life.

2110) Good or bad, right or wrong, all these things are perspectives-I get to pick which one I want so all I need to do is choose wisely.

2111) I am able to be both strong and sensitive, depending on the situation because masculine energy is not about being one or the other.

2112) I am not afraid of making mistakes because it is through them where I will learn what does and doesn't work for my personal growth.

2113) If I act like something is possible even if nobody else believes in it, then all this does is make what might be invisible visible.

2114) If someone says something unkind about me or tries to bring me down, I will not give them power by allowing their words to hurt me.

2115) Regardless of how much negativity surrounds me, all it means is that success is right around the corner so why would I give up now?

2116) Everything that happens in my life, I attract it. I know exactly what to do to create the kind of success and happiness that I want.

2117) Why should I believe anything other than success is possible when everything around here seems to be a constant manifestation of it?

2118) I am confident and secure in every aspect of life, including my relationships with friends, family, co-workers and romantic partners.

2119) No matter who I'm dealing with, the only thing that matters is my ability to handle their negativity in a positive way. I always win.

2120) While some people are busy being stuck where they are in life, I'm busy walking towards greatness regardless of how long it takes me.

2121) Why even bother asking questions when the answers are already inside of me? It's just a matter of whether or not I'm ready to listen.

2122) I am a man who creates his own luck because I take risks with everything, I do which means there is so much energy for me to draw upon.

2123) I know that if I trust myself, I will always have the best opportunities show up in my life because it is what makes me so successful.

2124) If something doesn't work out, that's no reason to become angry or bitter but simply a way for me to learn something new about myself.

2125) It's not about what happens to me, but how I react to it that matters most because this determines if things will get better or worse.

2126) Today is going to be a great day because whatever happens, I will face it with a big smile on my face and an outlook filled with hope.

2127) When I feel miserable, all I have to do is find one reason why that's good because then this misery will just disappear into thin air.

2128) My attitude determines my altitude. Every day, my attitude becomes more positive and productive as I help others reach their goals too.

2129) When others have more going on, this doesn't mean they deserve it-it just means their mindset allows them to create more opportunities.

2130) All that matters right now is being happy which means it's time to let go of all worries and negative thoughts because you are worth it.

2131) I am grateful for everything that comes into my mind each day because this means there are unlimited possibilities waiting for me ahead.

2132) My journey in life has been amazing so far and I know that there is nothing to stop me from achieving even greater success in my future.

2133) My journey today may be difficult but I am up for the challenge because I know that whatever doesn't kill me will only make me stronger.

2134) I am committed to turning my dreams into reality by following through with my goals each day until I get exactly what I want out of life.

2135) I am going to be successful in life no matter what because I have the courage and determination to face any obstacle that gets in my way.

2136) I am the only person who can make my life better so it's up to me and nobody else no matter how hard people try to convince me otherwise.

2137) All the energy anyone could ever need is available right here and right now so there's no reason to look for it in the past or the future.

2138) If someone has zero interest in what I have to offer, then that's just fine because there are plenty of women and people out there who do.

2139) Today is going to be a fantastic day because whatever happens, I will face it with a big smile on my face and an outlook filled with hope.

2140) Today is the day that I stop making excuses for myself because there are too many amazing things waiting to be discovered by me right now.

2141) I am always surrounded by opportunities for me to succeed no matter where I look because everything in life is only a reflection of myself.

2142) Any frustration or disappointment I'm feeling right now is always self-inflicted so there's no need for anyone else to give their two cents.

2143) Every day gets better than the last; each moment brings new insights, opportunities and experiences. My love increases more and more today.

2144) I am in control of the direction that my life takes because everything around me happens for a reason and is always working out in my favor.

2145) Like attracts like which means success loves company so if success isn't already showing up for me, then it's time for me to show up for it.

2146) The world around me may be loud, but I can drown it out by focusing on my thoughts which are always positive and encouraging no matter what.

2147) I enjoy every single minute in my life, because I know that this moment will never come back. And if it does, it will be in a different form.

2148) All of my fantasies are now coming true through whatever hard work I put into them so there is no doubt in my mind that anything is possible.

2149) I keep my body healthy. I eat only when hungry, drink only when thirsty, relax often, play hard, sleep long hours at night whenever possible.

2150) Making positive changes in my own life always inspires others to do the same, so I am constantly making a positive impact on those around me.

2151) Today I start with a clean slate and leave all past failures behind, no longer allowing them to influence who I want to become in the future.

2152) When I feel overwhelmed or distracted, this shows me where there needs to be improvement so all I need to do is push through and work harder.

2153) Everything around me is working in my favor. even if things might look difficult on the surface there are opportunities for growth everywhere.

2154) I am committed to living each day like it's my only one because life is too short for me to waste on things that don't matter in the long run.

2155) No matter how many times I fail in reaching a goal, tomorrow is another opportunity for me give it one more try until success greets me later.

2156) I am able to stand my ground and do what is right because I know that each of my actions will lead me towards the life that I am meant to live.

2157) If someone wants to judge me for whatever reason, why would I care? It's not like their opinion matters in any way so why let them ruin my day?

2158) I am not afraid of being successful because I know that it takes hard work, time and dedication to accomplish anything worthwhile in this world.

2159) Every single negative experience I've ever had in my entire life was completely and entirely determined by the thoughts I chose to focus on most.

2160) People can always see right through me and know whether or not I truly believe what I say because actions speak way louder than words ever could.

2161) For everything that happens to me, there is a valuable lesson buried beneath the surface-and learning from these lessons will only make me better.

2162) I trust that everything that has happened in the past has brought me to this moment so I can make a positive change. I am ready to succeed today.

2163) My past is behind me - it no longer has any influence on who I have become today because every day brings about new experiences and opportunities.

2164) Anything worth having requires dedication but what makes it even more difficult to achieve isn't the dedication itself but the discipline to do it.

2165) I am never upset with other people because of what they are doing, I'm only upset with them because of how their actions make me feel about myself.

2166) My thoughts are focused on creating a better future for myself and those around me – today is just the beginning of something great that lies ahead.

2167) I am the only one who can protect me from anything so no matter how hard someone else tries, they will always fail because I have all the power here.

2168) I release all worries and negative thoughts from my mind; letting go of the past allows me to focus on what really matters to move forward with ease.

2169) Dropping some pounds isn't just about looking better but it's also about being healthier too because there is nothing more important than my own life.

2170) In life, I am a creator and doer. In my mind is where the magic happens and my thoughts are what propel me forward towards more happiness and success.

2171) New doors are opening before me daily as new opportunities present themselves to part of my new journey. I will not miss any chance that comes my way.

2172) Happiness is a choice and it's a decision I make every single day when I wake up in order to be persistent in transforming any negatives into positives.

2173) I am capable of creating the future that I want for myself because I have done it before and know that there is nothing stopping me from doing it again.

2174) I prefer to be respected rather than liked because if everyone likes me, it doesn't actually say anything about me but simply means I have no standards.

2175) What other people think is none of my business because I can either take control or let someone else dictate how my life plays out. my choice is obvious.

2176) All of my thoughts are focused on what I want and where I'm going in life rather than what others are doing, what others have done or on life in the past.

2177) People who try to bring me down will continue to be miserable if they choose a path other than the one meant for them. This means only good things for me.

2178) Every minute spent with me is fun-filled and exciting, because I make everything around me more interesting than it was just before I arrived on the scene.

2179) I will accomplish far more than I set out to do because my thoughts are powerful and positive. My mind is focused on what needs to be done, not on failure.

2180) Successful people are attracted to me, because they can feel that I'm a man who lives a happy and fulfilling life.

2181) The greatest rewards in life don't always come with the least amount of effort but those who work hard deserve ALL of the credit for their accomplishments.

2182) All of my plans are coming together beautifully, better than I could have ever imagined. I am making positive changes that will bring me all that I desire.

2183) I am not afraid to ask for help from others because it is through the support and love of those around me that I will be able to accomplish my goals in life.

2184) I am unstoppable not because of who I am but because every single person only succeeds when they avoid giving up even when the odds are stacked against them.

2185) I create my own reality and if there is a situation that I don't want to be in, then it's simply because I'm not thinking about the possibilities where I am.

2186) I have no fear of rejection. I know that everything happens for a reason and that even though some doors are closed, better ones are opening up all the time.

2187) When someone betrays me or hurts me in some way, this simply means they have given up on being a good person so why hang onto them any longer than necessary?

2188) My emotions are telling me whether or not something is good for my growth because if it feels bad, it's generally a sign that something isn't working anymore.

2189) If people are having a more difficult time with something than what I am, this only means I've gotten better at whatever it is-I must be doing something right.

2190) I will always be the most powerful man in any room because no matter how much energy anyone else has, it's never even close to the energy that flows through me.

2191) There is no excuse for making the same mistake twice because this time, I will approach things with a totally different mindset which means nothing but success.

2192) No matter what happens, there is always something positive that comes out of any negative situation as long as I keep believing this until it becomes my reality.

2193) People like talking about other people because it gives them an opportunity to make themselves feel more significant or important than who they're talking about.

2194) The things people say to me don't have any power over me unless I give that power to them which means that negativity only has the power, I choose for it to have.

2195) I have amazing people in my life who are there to support me so why not reach out to someone today when you need help or just want to feel better about something?

2196) Opportunities may come and go but they are never lost because you always have an opportunity to create a new one that's just as good if not than the previous one.

2197) Today, I will accomplish far more than I set out to do because my thoughts are powerful and positive. My mind is focused on what needs to be done, not on failure.

2198) Anybody can smile on the outside even if they're dying inside which means it doesn't take much to fake happiness when your actual life is full of pain and suffering.

2199) I may not be able to change other people but there's nothing stopping me from changing myself which means who and what I am capable of becoming is entirely up to me.

2200) The past doesn't define who I am today so why should worries about what will happen in the future influence my current happiness? Live in the present moment instead.

Some Final Words

There are many challenges that men have to face in life.

Our modern society is not always kind to men, who are expected to meet an unrealistic ideal of what a man should be. There's pressure to be the soft, caring male, who is good at everything and has endless energy. You should be considerate, acknowledging and reserved, but when convenient you must be tough and are supposed to man up. With all this pressure, it's no wonder man often feel inadequate.

For your own sake it is important to cut out all this noise out there and discover a reality that is based on your intrinsic goals and values.

A man needs to know what he wants. He has to understand whatever it is that drives his passion, that makes him want to get up every morning and go the extra mile. He's got to think about what really matters in life. Only after he knows what his life goals are, should he decide how to act out.

A man needs to know himself - what makes him happy and fulfilled, what his talents are, the type of person that he wants to be in this world. And once he decides on all these things, only then can he start working towards them.

A man has to respect himself, before he can expect that

from someone else. Above all, a man needs to love himself. He needs to be able to go through life with confidence and self-awareness. Only then can he actually take action in his life.

As a man, it's up to you to define yourself - so don't waste your life following the wrong path. Your inner warrior wants to take control of your life and embrace what makes you unique, so that you can live a fulfilling life without regrets.

How about starting that journey right now? It is a journey that will change your life.

Feel free to contact us if you have any questions or suggestions:

relaxedgurubooks@gmail.com

Our books can't be successful without **your help**. It would mean the world to us if you could leave a **review on Amazon.**

Thank you!

Imprint / Impressum
Copyright © 2022 Greg Butcher
All rights reserved

Greg Butcher is represented by
Relaxed Guru Books
Bottrop
Relaxedgurubooks@gmail.com
ISBN: 9798412467962
Imprint: Independently published
Images: Licensed by Envato Elements

Printed in Great Britain
by Amazon

41537639R00118